SHOW ME HEAVEN

Donna L Taylor

Show Me Heaven
By Donna L Taylor

© Donna L Taylor

ISBN: 978-1-912092-32-1

First published in 2024

Published by Palavro, an imprint of
the Arkbound Foundation (Publishers)

Arkbound is a social enterprise that aims to promote social inclusion, community development and artistic talent. It sponsors publications by disadvantaged authors and covers issues that engage wider social concerns. Arkbound fully embraces sustainability and environmental protection. It endeavours to use material that is renewable, recyclable or sourced from sustainable forest.

Arkbound
Rogart Street Campus
4 Rogart Street
Glasgow, G40 2AA

www.arkbound.com

SHOW ME HEAVEN

Donna L Taylor

palavro
PUBLISHING

The publication of this book was enabled through a dedicated crowdfunding campaign on Crowdbound.org. Among the many supporters, we are particularly grateful to:-

Fawaz Suliman
Kevin Taylor
Mel Taylor
Ibrah Ikhter
Dr Ret Omoigui
Ivy Omari
Abdul Ssekajja
Israel Eweka
Ronke Idowu
Lydia Asamoah
Vida Sarpong
Dani Ungurusan

Acknowledgements

Firstly, I would like to thank my mother, my brother, Kevin and my amazing husband for supporting me with this book. My best friend, Kirsty, you are my rock. Heartfelt thanks go out to my cousin/surrogate brother, Mike Dewey, and life-long friends, Kay and Natashya. Thank you to my psychiatrist at Prospect Park Psychiatric Hospital for keeping me well, and to all those other awesome people who have helped me through my journey of mental illness—the list is too great to name them all individually.

I work with some really amazing, genuinely caring people who have done a great job in very difficult circumstances.

To others suffering as I have: Avoid becoming a revolving-door patient at all costs. Find, where possible, the medication you can tolerate and take it regularly. Avoid alcohol and illicit drugs, as both destroy lives and tear families apart. Don't act on suicidal thoughts—time passes, and things change. Life can go on.

Love, light and peace.

Dedicated to the memory of my brother, Mark Taylor

1st February, 1961 – 29th May, 2017

&

The memory of my mother, Norma Taylor

31st August, 1936 – 4th June, 2021

Contents

The following memoir is based on actual events. Only some of the names have been changed to protect individual identity.

"So stick to the fight when you're hardest hit –
It's when things seem worst that you must not quit."

An excerpt from Edgar A. Guest's poem, "Don't Quit."

Chapter One

The Memories

In the warm embrace of the sun, my earliest memories are a symphony of laughter and adventure in the sprawling garden of our seaside home in Skegness. Four young souls, my three brothers and I, found our paradise in this lush expanse, a place where imagination knew no bounds.

Mark, the eldest, always held a special place in my heart. He was my hero on many sunny afternoons, guiding my little tricycle through our garden adventures. Close behind, Gary, the second oldest with his light brown hair and deep brown eyes, and Kevin, our family's youngest charmer whose irresistible cuteness once captivated every mother in the maternity ward, navigated the skies with their model aeroplanes, adding a sense of thrill and wonder to our play.

In this idyllic setting, our loyal companion, Robbie—a spirited mix of German Shepherd and Labrador—was a constant presence. His barks of joy echoed our own, adding to the garden's lively atmosphere. Robbie shared a special bond with each of us, but our connection was unique. My most peaceful naps were spent on his comforting stomach, and Mum often recounted how he would patiently wait, motionless, until I awoke before rushing out to attend to his needs in the garden.

Robbie's gentle nature was evident, although he once found himself at the centre of a rather unexpected incident. When our postman accidentally stepped on his tail, Robbie's reaction led to a bite, spiralling into a court case. It was a tense time, but justice sided with our beloved pet, understanding the unintentional provocation he had faced.

These days, filled with innocence, laughter, and the unconditional love of a family and its four-legged member, painted my childhood in vibrant colours, each moment a treasured brushstroke on the canvas of my life.

Occasionally, a mischievous spirit would take hold of us and we'd find ourselves tiptoeing into the neighbour's garden. Here, a secret adventure unfolded as my brothers, agile as young monkeys, scaled the apple trees. Their laughter mingled with the rustling leaves as they shook the branches, sending apples tumbling down like sweet treasures at my feet. The taste of those stolen apples, so fresh and crisp, became a symbol of our childhood innocence—a taste as sweet and pure as those golden years that seemed endless in our young eyes.

In this tapestry of memories, my parents, Ted and Norma, stood as central figures, embodying the very essence of happiness and attractiveness. Mum, with her luscious jet black hair inherited from her father, and chestnut brown eyes that sparkled with life, had dimples that etched deep into her cheeks whenever she smiled. It was this radiant smile, I'm certain, that captured my dad's heart. And my dad, he was not to be outshined. Tall, with the slender grace of a young actor, his blonde hair and light blue eyes could remind one of a James Dean in his prime. Together, they formed a picture-perfect couple, their love story woven into the very fabric of our family's history.

In those early days, their harmony and love were the foundations of our home, a backdrop to the laughter and adventures that filled our days by the seaside. It was a time of innocence, joy, and familial love—a time that, in the eyes of a child, felt as if it would last forever.

The arrival of a daughter after a trio of boys took my Mum by complete surprise. Accustomed to the world of boys, she couldn't quite believe her eyes when I was born. It took the midwife to confirm the unexpected. Holding me up, my tiny, newborn form unmistakable, she had to reassure my mother with a gentle, "Mrs. Taylor, this is very much a girl!" That moment marked the beginning of a new chapter in our family's story, one filled with the joys and challenges of raising a girl amidst a band of brothers.

Mum's journey to this point had been one of modest beginnings. Growing up without much money, she found great joy and a sense of accomplishment in living in our large house, surrounded by acres of land. This home wasn't just a family residence; it was a realm of possibilities. Spare bedrooms were transformed into cosy spaces for bed and breakfast guests, offering a haven for holidaymakers during the bustling summer months. This venture wasn't just a source of pride for Mum; it was a vital supplement to the income she earned from her job at a local shop, where she diligently stacked vegetables, ensuring each display was perfect.

Dad's path, too, had its twists and turns. He spent his days as a long-distance lorry driver, a job that took him on journeys far and wide. But before the open road called to him, he ran his own business in Reading, delivering produce. It was in Reading where my story began, where I was born, setting the stage for the life that awaited me in the house by the seaside, the house that would become the canvas for my childhood memories.

Mum's roots lay in the quaint charm of a Hampshire bungalow, where life was simple yet filled with small joys. Her father, my grandad, was a familiar figure in the community as he drove the number 14 bus, a daily routine that connected him to the rhythms of the village. Mum, blessed with a beautiful singing voice, would often light up holiday camps with her performances, her melodies weaving through the air as she sang with friends.

It was during this time, amid the swirl of music and youthful dreams, that she met my dad. Their story began at a dance, a moment of serendipity that soon led them down the aisle, hand in hand, into a future they would build together. However, this newfound happiness faced a tragic turn. In a moment that sent ripples of sorrow through our family and the village, my Nan discovered the unimaginable: grandad had taken his own life by gassing himself with the oven. His choice to end his life in such a way, especially as he was known as a happy-go-lucky, outgoing man, left everyone in utter disbelief. This tragedy deeply affected Mum, shaking her to the core.

None of us, me or my siblings, ever got the chance to meet Grandfather Norman. His passing preceded the birth of any of his grandchildren. Yet, in the village of Alresford where he once lived, his memory was kept alive with fondness. People remembered him as "the salt of the earth", a man whose presence was a blessing to those around him. I often heard stories of his little jig dance, a simple act that brought laughter and joy to his family and friends. How I wished I could have seen that dance, to have shared a moment of laughter with him.

Today, a large photo frame sits prominently on my sideboard, capturing the essence of this kind, handsome, and proud man. It's a photograph taken on my mother's wedding day. In it, he is dressed in a fine suit, shirt, and tie, his attire completed with a flower buttonhole to mark the special occasion. This photograph, a frozen moment in time, is all I have to connect me to the grandfather I never met, a silent testament to a life that touched so many.

The fragile tapestry of our family life, woven with threads of hope and dreams, began to unravel in a way none of us could have anticipated. My Mum, who had once sought a haven of stability in her marriage, found her world turned upside down in a single, heart-wrenching moment. When I was just three years old, my dad, the man we thought would be our lifelong protector, vanished. He left without a word, swept away in the arms of another woman, leaving behind not just his family but a trail of secrets and debts.

The life we knew crumbled when it came to light that his business in Reading had collapsed, buried under a mountain of debt. The repercussions were immediate and devastating; we were on the brink of losing our home. My Mum, pregnant and with four young children to care for, found herself alone and destitute. The irony of our plight became more bitter when we learned that my father had found solace in the arms of a wealthy woman, surrounded by luxuries we could hardly imagine, like a private chef and gardener.

Confronted with this harsh reality, Mum's spirit fractured under the weight of despair. In a moment of overwhelming pain, she attempted to escape her sorrows, echoing the tragic choice of her own father. I, a mere toddler of three, stumbled upon this scene of desperation, awakening from my nap to find my mother unconscious, a policeman desperately trying to revive her.

Frozen in shock, my little voice called out, "Mummy. Mummy!" My arms reached for the embrace that had always been my sanctuary, but there was no response, no comforting warmth to envelop me. The piercing sound of an ambulance siren filled the air, signalling the end of an era. My mother was taken away, and with her departure, the golden age of my childhood slipped away, leaving a profound and irrevocable change in its wake.

***

As dawn broke, I found myself waking up in an unfamiliar bed, nestled in a room that was just as strange to me. Breakfast time brought me to a bustling room, echoing with the chatter of other kids, but a baffling sense of displacement clouded my young mind. I couldn't comprehend why I was here or why my older brothers were seated so distantly at another table. As I gazed down at the simple bowl of cornflakes before me, a wave of loneliness washed over me, and my eyes brimmed with tears. I longed to call out, "Where's Mummy?" but the words were trapped in my throat by a crushing blend of fear and confusion. Unable to express my turmoil, I dashed back to the safety of the bedroom, seeking solace under the cocoon of blankets.

During this perplexing time, my mother was receiving care in a psychiatric hospital, leaving us four children to navigate the unfamiliar environment of a children's home. Here, a rigid divide kept me apart from my brothers, who were housed in the boys' wing. Overwhelmed by anxiety, I found myself too petrified to speak or even eat. This worrying change in my behaviour prompted a visit from a doctor after a few days. He couldn't find anything medically amiss with me, yet no one took the time to gently unravel the mystery for a three-year-old heart, explaining where her mother was or the reasons behind her sudden absence.

Then, in a whirlwind of surprise, Mum returned. She stood at the entrance of the children's home, her arms wide open as if the world hadn't shifted beneath our feet. The noticeable change in her was the absence of her once-pregnant belly. The repercussions of a severe overdose and the ensuing medical care had tragically resulted in a miscarriage. With that, I not only lost a sibling but had also come perilously close to losing my mother.

Our reunion was a patchwork of emotions as we clambered into her quaint blue Austin 1100, hearts light with joy. I expected us to head home, but instead, our journey took an unexpected turn, leading us to my Nan's tiny Council flat in Reading. The space was limited, yet it felt like a haven. That night, us kids nestled together on the floor, wrapped in cosy blankets, while Mum claimed the sofa. The simplicity of the setup couldn't mask the relief and love that filled the room, a stark contrast to the uncertainty we had just left behind. However, the absence of our unborn sibling was an unspoken presence, adding weight to our family's reunion.

Nan, with her heart in the right place but her hands tied by the Council's housing rules, did her best to turn our stay at her one-bedroom flat into something bearable. She brought us jigsaw puzzles and teddy bears, hoping these small tokens of comfort would also keep us quiet, aware that the Council wouldn't look kindly upon four children crammed into her limited space. But children will be children, and our youthful energy soon spilt over, drawing complaints from the neighbours. Before long, social services were at the door, their faces a mix of shock and disapproval at our cramped living conditions. The inevitable happened: we were asked to leave, finding ourselves uprooted once more, this time to a bed and breakfast.

To my innocent eyes, this change seemed like an unexpected adventure. I was wide-eyed with wonder, thinking we were on holiday, especially when we were treated to fresh orange juice with breakfast—a luxury we seldom enjoyed. However, this illusion of a holiday was short-lived. Financial constraints soon forced us to move again, this time to a boarding house that was anything but welcoming. The place was a haven for the downtrodden and desperate; prostitutes and violent drunks were our nightly companions. Their loud arguments, filled with shouts and curses, became our unsettling lullabies as we huddled together on a mattress on the floor.

The atmosphere turned from unsettling to dangerous when Mum witnessed a horrific act of violence—a man brutally assaulting a woman. It was a stark, grim reminder that we were in a place no child should ever be. The final breaking point came one terrifying night when we heard someone fiddling with our door handle. It was a moment of pure fear, a clear signal that we weren't safe. With a sense of urgency, Mum decided we couldn't stay a moment longer. In the dead of night, we made our escape, clambering out of a window into the dark, ready to flee from the dangers that lurked within the walls of that boarding house.

Our last resort was the little Austin 1100, which now became our makeshift home. Mum and my brother Mark took the front seats while Gary and Kevin arranged themselves top to toe in the back. I squeezed into the only space left, the parcel shelf, pressing close to the rear windscreen. The sense of adventure had faded now; this no longer felt like a holiday, despite Mum's valiant attempts to keep our spirits high. As dawn broke, the harsh reality set in, especially for Mum, as curious passers-by glanced at us, the children sprawled asleep in the car. The humiliation she must have felt was beyond words. And then, our plight caught the eye of the press, turning our situation into a public spectacle as the story of a homeless single mother and her children living in a car spread across Reading.

Our story in the newspapers did, however, prompt action from the Council. We were quickly offered a house, which was a relief, regardless of its location in a less desirable part of town. Eager for a real home, we abandoned the Austin 1100. But our hearts sank as we saw our new residence. The house, part of a Victorian terrace, was not just rundown; it was condemned. The brickwork was decaying, and as we hesitantly entered, we were greeted by the foul odours of dampness and rodents.

That first night, we lay on the hard, bare floorboards, surrounded by flaking wallpaper. Mum did her best to keep our spirits up, but the reality was grim. The sound of mice scuttling in the darkness filled the silence, stirring a deep fear in me. Sleep was elusive as I lay there, wide-eyed, in our new, yet distinctly uninviting, home.

Mum, resilient and unyielding after all we had endured, refused to succumb to our dire circumstances. She took a significant step towards reclaiming some semblance of normalcy by securing a job as an administrator at the social services department in Reading.

This job wasn't just a means to an end; it became her anchor, her source of strength. Through every challenge, she showed up for work each day, embracing every opportunity for overtime. It provided her not just with financial security and a sense of stability, but I later came to understand that it also served as her sanctuary, a refuge from the complexities and struggles we faced at home.

Gradually, our dreary house started transforming. With Mum's steady income, we managed to buy some second-hand furniture, and rugs were laid over the cold, unforgiving floorboards. These small changes infused our home with a sense of warmth, making the space feel more like a haven for our battered spirits.

Despite the hardship she had experienced, Mum still longed for the support and stability that a partner could bring. Her heart, perhaps seeking comfort and normalcy, led her to someone new. However, this man was far from being the ideal stepfather figure. This development marked another chapter in our lives, intertwining hope with apprehension as Mum navigated her desire for companionship amidst our family's ongoing journey of resilience and survival.

Mum's encounter with Ray was as unexpected as it was transformative, beginning in the unassuming setting of a local pub where she sang. Ray was there, engaging in his preferred pastime: drinking. He was a charismatic Geordie with a nostalgic Teddy Boy quiff from the '50s, and his watery blue eyes often twinkled with sociability. When sober, Ray could be the kindest soul, generous to a fault. However, his battle with alcohol was a losing one; it eclipsed everything else in his life. His past was marked by a stint in the forces, but he had gone AWOL and even had brushes with the law, resulting in time in prison. Work was sporadic for him, taking a backseat to his dedication to alcohol.

Before long, Ray had become a permanent fixture in our home on Charles Street. While Mum tirelessly worked to support us, Ray turned our house into his personal social club, inviting friends over for day-long drinking sessions. He would start his mornings with spirits disguised in a mug, feigning it was tea to us kids. In dire times, he'd even resort to drinking aftershave for lack of money to buy proper spirits.

Nights were often filled with the sounds of Mum and Ray arguing, their disputes occasionally escalating to physical altercations. Despite the tumultuous and harmful nature of their relationship, Mum couldn't find it in herself to cast him out. The memory of her near-fatal experience when she was last alone haunted her, making the thought of solitude more frightening than the chaos Ray brought into our lives.

Ray's presence cast a shadow over our family life, but it was Kevin, my youngest brother, who seemed to bear the brunt of the strain. The tension between him and Ray was palpable, leading to constant friction and arguments. The situation grew so intolerable for Kevin that he saw no other option but to escape it. In a mix of desperation and defiance, he made the heartbreaking decision to run away.

Kevin's escape to the local park was a child's attempt at finding solace and control in an uncontrollable world. He crafted a makeshift den from branches and leaves, a small fortress in his eyes, before returning to fetch me for company. My steps were hesitant, filled with mixed emotions, as I took his hand and followed him back to his leafy hideout. There, under the makeshift canopy now heavy with rainwater, I found myself caught between two worlds: the chaotic home on Charles Street and this damp, makeshift shelter in the park.

Sitting there, the sound of raindrops pattering above us, I turned to Kevin with a thought. "Kevin," I whispered, "You know Mum's got sausages for tea." I knew his fondness for them, and I watched the internal battle play out on his face. The choice was stark: the comfort of his favourite meal or the harsh reality of life in our dilapidated house, overshadowed by the presence of an angry, drunken stepfather.

After a moment of contemplation, his resolve wavered. "Alright then, I'll come back," he said, the reluctance in his voice mirroring the conflict within. We walked back to Charles Street, unnoticed in our brief absence. But that night, Kevin expressed his silent defiance and deep-seated resentment in a poignant gesture. He etched "I hate Ray" into the headboard of my mother's bed, a quiet yet powerful testament to the turmoil and anguish he felt. It was a child's way of screaming into the void, a desperate plea for change in our tumultuous lives.

***

Our lives took a turn for the better three or four years after Mum and Ray became a couple, when the Council finally allocated us a proper house. It was part of a new development on Blithe Walk in south Reading. As luck would have it, the builders were just wrapping up, and Mum had the privilege of choosing our new home. She selected number eight, a choice that filled us with a sense of hope and anticipation for a new beginning.

Our new abode at 8 Blithe Walk was modest yet represented a world of improvement. It featured three bedrooms, fitted carpets, and even a small back garden, though devoid of grass, as the Council had decided against providing it. Mark and I shared the second bedroom, while Kevin and Gary occupied the box room with its bunk beds.

However, our move didn't leave all our troubles behind. The friction between Kevin and Ray only intensified, paralleled by a worsening in Ray's drinking habits. Ray's addiction led him to desperate measures, like selling our possessions without Mum's knowledge to fund his alcoholism. One day, Mum returned to discover the fridge-freezer gone, traded away by Ray for money to quench his thirst.

My escape from the turmoil of 8 Blithe Walk was my local

primary school, a 20-minute walk away, near my Nan's tiny Council flat. Every Tuesday and Thursday, I would go to Nan's for tea, and those afternoons became my sanctuary. There, in the warmth of her home, I found solace and joy. Nan would cook my favourite meal: faggots, chips, and peas. She indulged my childish whims, letting me dress up in her old high heels, unused due to her arthritis, and drape myself in her costume jewellery. We would then sit down to our humble feast, and she would entertain me with stories of the war, of times when they were bombed out by a doodlebug. Those moments with Nan were precious, a brief respite from the challenges at home, filled with love, warmth, and a connection to a past that seemed so much simpler than my present, and I would try to stretch them for as long as I could. But inevitably, the time would come for me to leave. Nan would gently nudge, "I think it's time to go home now, love." With a heavy heart, I would take off the costume jewellery and shoes, don my coat, and start the slow, reluctant walk home. Each step was filled with dread, silently hoping that I wouldn't return to find our house engulfed in another of Ray's and Mum's fiery arguments.

One chilly Tuesday in October, when I was about 11 years old, I hurried back from school to Nan's flat, eager to escape the biting cold. Nan, ever thoughtful despite her painful arthritis, always left a key on a string through the letterbox for me. This meant I could let myself in without troubling her to answer the door. I reached in and retrieved it. As I turned the key in the lock and pushed open the creaky front door of Nan's flat, a sense of foreboding gripped me. It was a feeling I couldn't quite place at first, like a shadow lurking in the corners of my mind.

The door swung open with a low groan, revealing a dimly lit hallway. The air felt heavy, laden with a silent anticipation that prickled the hairs on the back of my neck. I glanced down the corridor, the doorway to the front room standing ajar, beckoning me with a sense of dread. My heart pounded in my chest as I stepped forward, each footfall echoing in the quietude of the flat.

There, in the gloom of the front room, lay my Nan. She was fully clothed, her frail form sprawled on the floor, an eerie stillness enveloping her. The sight struck me like a blow to the stomach, stealing the breath from my lungs.

Confusion and concern washed over me as I approached her. "Nan! What are you doing?" I asked, kneeling down to rouse her.

I shook her arm gently, but there was no response. Her skin was alarmingly cold. In a rush of worry, I removed my winter coat and draped it over her, hoping to warm her somehow. Then, with shaking hands, I ran to the phone and dialled 999.

"My Nan's not moving, and she feels cold," I stammered into the receiver, my voice a blend of fear and urgency. "I think she's ill."

The voice on the other end was calm and reassuring. "Just stay on the phone," they instructed. "We'll get someone out to you as soon as possible."

In those tense, agonising moments, waiting for help to arrive, the reality of the situation began to sink in. The comforting afternoons at Nan's, the stories, the laughter, and the dress-up—all suddenly seemed so fragile, so precious, and perhaps, perilously close to becoming memories.

The kind lady on the phone kept me engaged in conversation, a soothing presence until the ambulance arrived. They swiftly took my Nan to the hospital, leaving me in a state of confusion and worry. It was only later, in the gentle, sombre tones of my Mum's voice, that the heart-wrenching truth was revealed to me. My beloved Nan hadn't been asleep; she had had a massive heart attack, right there in the hallway in front of the main door, that had ultimately taken her life. The realisation that I had been futilely trying to warm her lifeless body was a shock that deeply affected me.

The subsequent week was a blur of grief and tears. I watched, heartbroken, as Nan's coffin was slowly lowered into the earth. She was finally reunited with her husband, their tombstone bearing a poignant message, "This is not goodbye, my darling— just goodnight." But to me, it felt like a final farewell, a devastating closure.

Nan's passing felt like the crumbling of my world. She was not just my darling grandmother but also my sanctuary, my respite from the chaotic life at home. With her gone, it felt as though I had lost more than just a loved one; I had lost my safe haven, my escape. The troubles at home, which I could momentarily forget in Nan's loving company, now loomed larger and more insurmountable than ever. In her absence, I found myself facing a stark reality with nowhere else to turn, longing for the warmth and love that had been my solace.

The memory of Nan's words, spoken just three days before her passing, echoed hauntingly in my mind. For months, she had shared with Mark and me about a recurring dream she had. In these dreams, she was endlessly searching for her beloved husband, Norman. It was a journey she embarked on night after night in her sleep, a testament to the depth of her love and longing. Remarkably, just before her death, she had finally found him in her dream. They were reunited at last, a serene and joyful conclusion to her nocturnal quest. Then, only a few days later, she left us in reality, perhaps to join him in a place beyond dreams.

In the midst of this poignant moment, I remembered a special bond that Nan, Mark, and I shared; a poem we had written together. This poem was more than just words on paper; it was a symbol of our connection, a creative expression of the love and memories we shared. The verses we crafted together now held even more significance, a lasting tribute to Nan's influence in our lives and the unbreakable bond we had formed.

The poem, a simple yet profound creation, was a reflection of our collective experiences, dreams, and the love that bound us. It was a testament to the legacy Nan left behind, not just in her passing but in the lessons she taught us and the warmth she brought to our lives. In those words, we found comfort, a reminder of her spirit and the timeless nature of the love we shared.

The Christmas Toast

Christmas comes just once a year.
It`s full of happiness & good cheer.
We should remember when we drink the wine.
Whose birthday it is at Christmas time.

He died on the cross his life he gave.
To all good people he did save.
A crown of thorns was placed on his head.
He hung on the cross until he was dead.

This was a time for sadness & sorrow.
For no one knows what will happen tomorrow.
So, when you raise your glasses up high.
Drink to the man who was willing to die.

Recalling "The Christmas Toast" poem brings back a flood of vivid memories, especially of the time when I recited it aloud in my class at school. It's remarkable how certain words, once spoken or heard, can imprint themselves indelibly in our minds. For me, that poem, learned and recited at the tender age of 11, has remained a cherished memory, an emblem of a significant moment in my life.

The poem, with its festive theme and heartfelt words, was more than just a verse to be spoken; it was a piece of my history, a connection to a time and place that shaped who I am. Reciting it in class was not just a school exercise but a personal journey, a moment where I could share a part of myself and my story with others.

To this day, the lines of "The Christmas Toast" linger in my memory, a testament to the impact of words and the power of poetry to encapsulate emotions, memories, and experiences. It serves as a reminder of my youth, my family, and the enduring presence of those who have touched my life in profound ways.

Chapter Two

The Teenage Years

As we all moved into our teens, the trauma of our childhoods began to play out in different ways.

Mark's transformation was profound and deeply unsettling. Once a vibrant presence in the family, he now became a shadow of his former self, retreating into the sanctuary of his bedroom. This became his refuge, a place where he could shut out all the noises of the outside world. Inside these four walls, he would while away the hours in solitude, a cigarette between his fingers, the smoke swirling and dissipating into the dim light. His passion for the outside world had dwindled to a singular interest: fishing. He would sit by the river's edge, alone, for countless hours, his line cast into the rippling waters. It was a silent pursuit, one that mirrored his internal state; calm on the surface, yet with undercurrents of turmoil.

My brother, once the favourite, had become a stranger, his once-lively spirit dimmed by the weight of depression and seclusion. He had receded from our lives, his presence a mere whisper of what it once was.

In stark contrast, Gary's response to our familial strife was to hurl himself into the outside world with abandon. He found solace and identity among the mods, a subculture defined by their sleek style and love for scooters. He acquired a moped, an emblem of his newfound belonging, and could often be seen zipping through the streets of Scarborough. The hum of the engine and the rush of wind became his escape, a way to distance himself from the chaos at home. At least, he was building a social life, a tapestry of friendships and adventures, highlighting the difference in his and Mark's personalities.

But it was Kevin, our youngest brother, whose path caused the deepest concern. I didn't blame him for veering into a dangerous trajectory and aligning himself with the skinhead movement. He'd had a turbulent time growing up with Ray, making it his life's mission to pick on him. Even then, his descent into the world of drugs was rapid and alarming. Cannabis was merely the gateway; soon, he was ensnared by the destructive embrace of heroin. Our home, already besieged by the shadows of alcoholism, now harboured a more sinister spectre: drug addiction. Kevin's journey into this dark abyss marked a new chapter of turmoil in our family, one that threatened to unravel the fragile threads that held us together.

Each of us had found our unique means of survival, a way to navigate the stormy seas of our family life. I sought refuge in the comforting arms of my Nan's home, a sanctuary where the chaos of our house seemed a distant echo. Her place was a haven, where the warmth of her presence and the tranquillity of her home provided a stark contrast to the disarray I left behind.

While Mum, ever resilient, immersed herself in her work. It was her escape, a realm where she could exert control and find a sense of normalcy amidst our domestic upheaval. Work became her solace, a place where she could don the armour of professionalism and temporarily shed the burdens of her personal life.

Mark, in his own way, chose isolation as his shield. He retreated into his private world, a realm where he could erect walls to keep the pain and chaos at bay. In his seclusion, he found a bitter kind of peace, a respite from the storm raging outside his door.

But the struggles of Kevin and Ray brought an unwelcome spotlight to our home. The frequent visits from the police turned our house into a landmark of notoriety in the neighbourhood. The local kids, once friendly and curious, now whispered cautions to each other, casting our home as a place to avoid. "Don't go round to number eight. The coppers are always there," they'd say, their words tinged with a mix of fear and fascination. This reputation only added to the sense of isolation and stigma we felt, further alienating us from the community we once felt a part of. Our home, which should have been a sanctuary, had now become a spectacle for everyone.

At the tender age of 15, I managed to find a sliver of independence in a modest cleaning job. The work was humble, but it offered me something invaluable: a sense of autonomy. Each pay check was a small victory, a testament to my own effort and resilience. With a heart full of aspirations, I began to save my hard-earned wages, dreaming of a luxury that had always been beyond my reach: gold jewellery.

This wasn't just about adornment; it was a symbol of self-worth, a tangible proof that I could carve out something beautiful in my otherwise chaotic world. After months of diligent saving, I finally purchased those gleaming trinkets, each piece a sparkling beacon of my determination and independence.

However, my joy was brutally short-lived. One fateful day, I returned home to discover a shattering truth: our house had been burgled. The sanctuary I had known was violated, its privacy shattered. And there, amidst the disarray and the feeling of violation, was the stinging realisation that my treasured jewellery, my symbol of hope and hard work, was gone.

The police arrived, their presence a familiar yet unwelcome part of our family narrative. Their investigation led to a chilling conclusion: the perpetrator had access to our house key. In that moment, as Mum and I exchanged a silent, knowing glance, a heavy weight of understanding settled between us. This theft was not a random act; it was tied to the very fabric of our family's struggles.

We didn't need to voice our thoughts; they hung in the air, heavy and unspoken. The jewellery, like so many things before, had vanished into the void of our family's troubles. And now, a haunting question lingered: was it Ray, driven by his need for alcohol, or Kevin, ensnared in his drug addiction? The uncertainty was a bitter pill, adding a layer of mistrust and suspicion to our already burdened lives. The theft of my jewellery was not just a loss of possessions; it was a poignant reminder of the deep fractures within our family, a symbol of the sacrifices and pain that came with loving those who were losing themselves to their demons.

Every step I took towards happiness seemed to crumble beneath me, as if the universe conspired to strip me of any joy I dared to grasp. It was during this tumultuous phase of my life that I crossed paths with my first boyfriend, Patrick, a vision straight out of an Irish fairytale. With his piercing blue eyes that shimmered like the ocean on a sunny day and his blond hair that cascaded with a golden sheen, he was the epitome of my teenage dreams; a living, breathing doppelgänger of Simon Le Bon from the iconic band, Duran Duran.

Patrick was the talk of the town, his popularity unmatched, his charm undeniable. So, when he confessed his fancy for me, it felt like a fantasy unfolding. I was elated, in disbelief, and utterly swept off my feet. But as quickly as this euphoria arrived, it was shadowed by the creeping tendrils of my past.

The traumas that had lain dormant in the recesses of my childhood began to stir, emerging like spectres to haunt my present. They wrapped their cold fingers around my happiness, turning it to ash. My brother Mark, a mirror of my own struggles, was sinking into the depths of depression, and I found myself being dragged down alongside him. The weight of these dark emotions was crushing.

On the days Patrick asked me out, my heart ached to say yes, to leap into the possibility of love and laughter. But more often than not, I found myself imprisoned by a melancholy so deep that I couldn't muster the strength to face the world outside. In desperation, I turned to Natashya, my school friend, imploring her to be my messenger. She would relay excuses to Patrick—tales of illness, commitments, anything to mask the truth of my despair.

As time trickled by, the inevitable happened. The gorgeous Patrick, with his heart of gold and spirit of adventure, found himself drawn to another. I watched, heartbroken, as he slipped through my fingers like grains of sand, leaving me to grapple with the bitter truth. I had lost him, a casualty of my own battles, a loss that I alone had orchestrated. It was a lesson etched in pain, a reminder of the price of letting the shadows of the past dictate the possibilities of the future.

In that moment, gradually yet irrevocably, I crossed the threshold into a shadowy realm I had no name for. Depression, that looming figure in the shadows, had enveloped me in its silent grasp, though I lacked the words or understanding to identify it. If you had inquired about the nature of this affliction, I would have been at a loss for an answer. All I comprehended was the overwhelming lethargy that anchored me to my bed, transforming my room into a solitary refuge where time seemed to stand still. The sun would rise and set, yet I remained cocooned in my own world of inertia, surfacing only for fleeting moments during meals.

Natashya, ever concerned, would often probe gently, her voice laced with worry, seeking to understand the invisible weight that kept me chained to my bed in my self-imposed isolation. Her questions echoed in the emptiness of my understanding, for I had no answers to give. This unknowable void within me was as much a mystery to myself as it was to her.

My absence at school became a constant, so much so that

my name no longer echoed in the classrooms during roll call. The void I left was met with silence, not inquiry. There were no concerned visits from the education department, no probing questions about my prolonged absence. It seemed as though they, too, had resigned themselves to the narrative of a troubled child from a fractured home, expecting nothing more than the path of least resistance; a descent into oblivion.

In this chapter of my life, I drifted through days blurred together, a ghost in my own existence, unseen and unheard, a young soul caught in the grips of an unseen adversary, struggling silently in the depths of an unnamed darkness.

As the critical time of my O-Levels approached, the shadow of my prolonged absence loomed large. The final year of school, with its myriad lessons and milestones, had slipped through my fingers like sand, leaving me unprepared and adrift. The thought of facing these pivotal exams was akin to confronting a vast, insurmountable wall with no footholds in sight.

With a heart heavy with resignation, I mustered the courage to attend a couple of the exams. Yet, as I sat in the hushed exam hall, the questions before me might as well have been written in an indecipherable script. My pen hovered motionless over the paper, my mind as blank as the sheet staring back at me. The ticking clock in the room was a stark reminder of time slipping away, ungrasped and unutilised.

When the ordeal of exams drew to a close, a flicker of hope ignited within me. I approached the head teacher, my voice trembling with a mix of fear and hope, to request the possibility of retaking the year. However, the response was a resounding no, a door firmly closed. It seemed the school had no inclination to peel back the layers of my struggles or offer a lifeline in the form of a second chance. They appeared more than ready to wash their hands of me, another troublesome element tied to a "troubled family", best forgotten and left behind.

The rejection was a bitter pill, leaving me to grapple with the realisation that my academic path, once filled with potential, had veered off course, derailed by a series of unseen, unspoken challenges. I was left standing at a crossroads, with the school fading into the distance, a symbol of lost opportunities and unyielding systems.

At that juncture, my life seemed to be slipping away, vanishing like a ghostly wisp into the fog of uncertainty and despair. The haunting ghost of my brothers' paths loomed ominously in my mind, a grim reminder of the potential fate that could befall me. Even more chilling was the thought of succumbing to an act of utter desperation, a path tragically trodden by my grandad and Mum. It felt as if I were teetering on the brink of an abyss, the darkness of hopelessness beckoning.

Yet, in this lowest point of my existence, at the very edge of surrender, an unexpected resilience surged within me. It was a fierce, raw defiance, a kindling of spirit that refused to be extinguished. This defiance was not just for myself, but against the myriad forces that seemed to conspire against us—the father figures who had abandoned their roles, leaving voids filled with disillusionment; the teachers who had given up on us, their dismissive attitudes sealing our fates in their minds; and the relentless shadows of poverty, grub, and violence that had been constant, uninvited companions in our lives.

In this moment of profound clarity, a resolve took root. I was determined not to let the turbulent currents of my circumstances drag me into the depths. This inner rebellion was a silent proclamation that I would not be another casualty of a system and a society that seemed all too ready to let me fall through the cracks. It was a vow to myself, a promise forged in the fires of adversity, that I would rise, fight, and carve a path distinct from the sorrow-laden trails left by those before me.

Summoning every ounce of determination I had left, I

wrenched myself from the grasp of my bed, a symbolic act of breaking free from the chains of despair that had bound me for so long. Standing before the mirror, I scrubbed my face, as if washing away not just the physical remnants of my tumultuous past but also the psychological scars that had marred my spirit.

Clad in a newfound resolve, I stepped out to face the world again, this time for an interview at the Intervention Board for Agricultural Produce. The position was for an administrative role, a realm far removed from the chaos that had engulfed my life. In my heart, I clung to the hope that work had been the anchor that had kept Mum steady amidst life's storms. Perhaps it could serve as my lifeline too.

The interview room was a world apart from the shadows I had been inhabiting. As I sat there, answering questions and trying to project a sense of confidence I scarcely felt, I was acutely aware of my lack of qualifications, the gaping holes in my academic journey.

Reflecting on that pivotal moment, it stands out in my memory as a blend of nerves and excitement—a cocktail of emotions that marked the beginning of a new chapter. It was my very first interview, a milestone in its own right, and the anticipation of it had sent waves of nervous energy coursing through me. Every question posed, every answer given, was tinged with the hope and anxiety of making that first impression count.

Despite the butterflies in my stomach and the rapid beating of my heart, there was an underlying thrill, a sense of adventure in stepping into the unknown. And then, the moment of truth arrived—the job offer. It was a victory, not just in securing employment, but in overcoming my own fears and uncertainties.

So in an unexpected turn of fate, they hired me.

The joy and relief that washed over me upon hearing I got the job are indescribable. It wasn't just about the role itself; it was the recognition, the chance to prove myself, and the opportunity to embark on a journey of personal and professional growth.

That mix of nervousness and exhilaration became a cherished memory, a reminder of where I started and how far I had come. I now had a chance to rebuild, to forge a new identity beyond the confines of a "troubled family". In that moment, I realised that sometimes, amidst the rubble of broken dreams, new opportunities can arise, offering a path to redemption and a chance to redefine one's destiny.

The job I had landed at the Intervention Board for Agricultural Produce was, by no measure, glamorous or particularly well-paying. Its nature was mundane, the tasks often monotonous, blending one day into the next in a tapestry of routine. Yet, in this simplicity, I found an unexpected solace.

The essence of my role was encapsulated in the meticulous handling of A3 yellow forms, known officially as C12-20s. These documents were the lifeblood of my daily tasks, each form a vital link in the complex chain of agricultural exports. My responsibilities extended beyond the mere completion of paperwork; I was the middle-man between the agricultural heartlands and the regulatory frameworks that governed them. This entailed regular communication with farmers, the custodians of the land who toiled to feed nations, and the officials at HM Revenue & Customs, the guardians of the country's fiscal policies and regulations.

Stationed in an office dubbed "Refund Control", my work revolved around a crucial financial lifeline for the farming community. We managed the refunds allocated to farmers for their efforts in exporting produce to third world countries, a noble endeavour aimed at supporting global food security and aiding those in less fortunate regions. This task was not just administrative but carried a weight of social responsibility, ensuring that the farmers were reimbursed for their contributions to this international cause.

The job, though seemingly straightforward, was a delicate

balancing act. It required an understanding of agricultural practices, empathy towards the hardworking farming community, and a meticulous attention to detail in navigating the bureaucratic intricacies of tax regulations. Every completed C12-20 form represented a successful transaction, a small victory in the broader mission of fostering global agricultural support and cooperation.

The job bestowed upon me a semblance of normality, a structure to my days that had been absent for so long. It became the reason I found the strength to leave the confines of my bed each morning, a small yet significant victory against the shadows that had enveloped my life.

Despite this newfound routine, the battle with my inner demons was far from over. Depression, like a persistent fog, still clouded many of my days, anchoring me in place, unable to face the world outside. There were mornings when the weight of my own thoughts made the journey to work insurmountable. Yet, as time passed, these days of immobilising despair began to stop, slowly but perceptibly.

It was a gradual journey, stretching over two long years, a path marked with small steps and occasional stumbles. Along this journey, I redefined what 'normal' meant for me. This new normal was not the absence of challenges, but the ability to navigate through them amidst the continuing chaos of my home life. It was a normalcy that acknowledged the scars of the past while steadily moving towards a future that I was actively shaping, a future that once seemed as distant as a mirage but was now slowly crystallising into reality.

At the age of 18, having built a sense of resilience and a few years of administrative experience under my belt, I began to cast my gaze towards new horizons. The "modest" salary from my current role had me perpetually tethered to my overdraft, a financial tightrope that left little room for stability or growth. It was time for a change, a step up to a role that not only offered better compensation but also promised a pathway to future advancement.

My search led me to The Prudential, a notable giant in the corporate world, known for its stability and growth opportunities. There, I found a listing for an administrative role similar to my own but with the promise of a significantly better salary. The prospect of working for such a reputable company was enticing, not just for the financial uplift but for the potential career pathways it could open up.

This was only my second job application, yet the alignment between the job requirements and my own skills filled me with a newfound confidence. My tenure in my first job had equipped me with a robust set of administrative skills—letter writing, form completion, telephone communication, filing, and computer proficiency. I could now bring tangible experience to the table, a fact that bolstered my confidence as I prepared for the interview.

The position initially implied a relocation to Holborn, London, with the promise of moving to the Pension Administration Team in Forbury Gardens, Reading, in the near future. However, destiny had other plans, and instead, I found myself embarking on a journey with the Ordinary Branch Life Assurance Surrender Claim Payments team. My role here was multifaceted, involving the precise task of stamping claim numbers on files and meticulously separating documents for distribution. I was responsible for generating the necessary paperwork for cheque issuance by the cashiers and creating claim files—a critical function that underscored the importance of accuracy and attention to detail.

Filing became a significant part of my daily routine, along with sorting post and delving into archived microfilm details. This aspect of the job required me to navigate the historical records of policies, discerning whether a death, surrender, or maturity claim had been paid, or if a policy had lapsed due to non-payment of premiums. Each file told a story of its own, with outcomes ranging from policies acquiring a paid-up value for future claims to lapsing without any value, a stark reminder of the real-life implications of our work.

In addition to these tasks, I was charged with the urgent delivery of surrender cheque requests to the cashiers, alongside a spectrum of other administrative duties. Each day brought its own set of challenges and learning opportunities, immersing me in the intricate workings of life assurance and the critical role of administrative support in facilitating the company's operations. This position not only honed my existing skills but also expanded my understanding of the insurance sector, laying the groundwork for my professional growth within the industry.

Securing the position at The Prudential was a moment of triumph that marked a significant turning point in my career and personal development. The excitement of this new opportunity invigorated me, and I dove into my work with a zeal that was driven by a desire to showcase my potential beyond the routine tasks assigned to me. I was not content with being pigeonholed as merely a proficient filer or administrator; I yearned to demonstrate the depth of my capabilities.

Yet, amidst this drive to excel and make my mark, I was acutely conscious of the limitations imposed by my lack of formal qualifications. This awareness became the catalyst for a transformative decision in my career path: I decided to further my education through the opportunities provided by my employer. The Prudential offered programs for employees to gain industry-recognised qualifications, and I seized this chance with both hands, embarking on a course of study that would pave the way for me to become a financial advisor.

This decision to pursue further qualifications was not taken lightly. It represented a commitment to personal and professional growth, a tangible step towards transcending the barriers that my earlier educational interruptions had imposed on me. Studying for these exams required discipline, dedication, and a balancing act between my job responsibilities and educational aspirations. But the prospect of becoming a financial advisor filled me with a sense of purpose and direction that I had not felt in years.

With each page of study material turned, each concept mastered, and each exam passed, I could feel the foundations of my future career being laid. This was more than just academic achievement; it was a personal quest to redefine my identity and capabilities. The path I had chosen was challenging, yet it was imbued with a determination and focus that had been rekindled within me, driving me towards a future where I could not only advise and guide others in their financial decisions but also stand as a testament to the power of resilience and self-improvement.

Chapter Three

The Love Life

The shift towards a more positive outlook on life seemed to be a catalyst for change in more areas than just my professional ambitions. For years, my personal life, particularly my romantic interactions, had been stifled by the shadow of depression that loomed large over my teenage years. Social outings were few and far between, and the idea of dating seemed like a distant, almost alien concept. However, as I began to find my footing, both in my career and my studies, the world around me started to brighten, offering glimpses of possibilities I had not dared to imagine before.

It was during an evening out at a pub in Reading, an event that would have been unthinkable had I still been in my darker days, that life surprised me with an unexpected twist. I was there with a friend, enjoying the simple pleasure of being out, surrounded by the buzz of conversation and laughter, when a chance encounter shifted the course of my evening. A couple of lads, acquaintances of my friend, joined us. And amidst the casual introductions and exchange of pleasantries, I found myself the focus of one of them.

He was tall and dark, a striking figure with a presence that commanded attention. His brown eyes twinkled with a kind of confidence and charm that felt both alluring and intimidating. It was an attraction that seemed worlds away from the uncertainties that had defined so much of my life. His name was Tony, and as we conversed, I found myself drawn into the ease of his company, his words weaving a spell of interest and attraction that I was unaccustomed to.

The conversation between us flowed effortlessly, and before I fully comprehended the gravity of the moment, I had agreed to go on a date with him. This agreement marked a significant departure from my usual introversion and self-imposed isolation. Tony, with his assured demeanour and engaging conversation, represented not just a personal connection but a symbol of the new chapters that were beginning to unfold in my life. It was a step into the unknown, a foray into the world of dating that I had nearly resigned myself to never experiencing. Yet, here I was, on the cusp of something new and exhilarating, a testament to the unexpected turns life can take when one starts to embrace change and open up to the possibilities it presents.

Tony's gestures of affection, marked by the regular arrival of flowers and chocolates at my doorstep, became highlights in our budding relationship. Each bouquet and box of sweets not only endeared him further to me but also to my mother, who found joy and perhaps a hint of vicarious romance in these acts of thoughtfulness. Watching her arrange the flowers with a contented smile, I could sense her approval and hope.

"This Tony's great, isn't he?" she remarked, her voice carrying a warmth that had been absent for too long, as she delicately placed the latest blooms in a vase on the kitchen table. To her, Tony represented a stark contrast to the parade of disappointments and mistreatment she had endured from men throughout her life. In her eyes, and perhaps in reality too, Tony was something of an angel; a beacon of kindness and respect in a world that had often shown her the opposite.

Even Ray, whose judgments were usually reserved and hard-won, seemed to hold a favourable opinion of Tony. His presence brought a semblance of normalcy and happiness into our home, a phenomenon we were all unaccustomed to but eagerly welcomed.

For me, Tony's allure was not just in his romantic gestures but also in the stability and ambition he represented. He had a steady job as an electrician, working within his dad's small property development company. This aspect of his life spoke volumes about his reliability and work ethic—traits that were both reassuring and attractive. In a world where my experiences with men were limited and often shadowed by the tumultuous relationships witnessed at home, Tony's consistency and kindness shone brightly.

I found myself in agreement with my mother's and Ray's assessments. Tony did seem pretty perfect. His actions, coupled with his steady employment, painted a picture of a future that was both hopeful and exciting. It was a blossoming romance that promised not just personal happiness but also a sense of familial approval and support that had been sorely missing.

The allure of Tony extended beyond the tangible expressions of affection that he so thoughtfully provided; it was deeply rooted in the familial environment he introduced me to—an environment I had longed for throughout my life. Tony's family presented a picture of stability and warmth that was alien to my own experiences. The foundation of his family was built on a marriage that had stood the test of time, a concept that felt both novel and deeply comforting to me. His parents, still together, exuded a sense of partnership and mutual respect that I had only ever dreamed of, and his siblings welcomed me with open arms, treating me as if I were already a member of their tight-knit circle.

Our weekends spent together at the pub for Sunday lunch became the highlights of my week, embodying moments of pure contentment and belonging. These gatherings were marked by laughter, shared stories, and a sense of camaraderie that I had never known. The absence of excessive drinking or arguments, so common in my own familial experiences, made these occasions seem all the more idyllic. For the first time, I witnessed what a supportive and loving family dynamic looked like in practice, and it was nothing short of blissful.

Immersed in this new environment, I began to envision a future for myself that was interwoven with Tony's family. The possibility of being part of a unit that was characterised by love, support, and stability filled me with hope and a sense of aspiration that had been missing from my life. It wasn't just about escaping the challenges of 8 Blithe Walk; it was about moving towards a future that promised the kind of familial warmth and security I had always craved. Tony and his family offered me a glimpse into a life that was not defined by strife but by the possibility of happiness and belonging, and I found myself dreaming of a day when I could truly call that world my own.

The moment that would pivot the direction of my life arrived sooner than expected, catching me off guard on an ordinary day just after my 19th birthday. The sun had barely crept above the horizon, casting a soft, golden glow that seemed to beckon new beginnings, when Tony appeared at the doorstep. But this visit was unlike any before; his arms cradled not just the vibrant hues of fresh flowers but a promise, a hope, encased within the delicate embrace of a small, velvet box.

As he knelt before me, the world around us seemed to pause, holding its breath in anticipation. The air was filled with a palpable tension, laced with the sweet scent of the blooms he held, as he opened the box to reveal a solitaire diamond ring. The gem caught the morning light, scattering it in a thousand different directions, each sparkle a testament to the magnitude of the moment. The band was of yellow gold, simple yet elegant, a perfect embodiment of the promise it was meant to symbolise.

"Donna," Tony's voice broke through the silence, his words carrying the weight of his emotions, "will you marry me?" He spoke of a future, painted with broad strokes of hope and dreams. "My dad's found this charming little house near Prospect Park. It's not without its quirks, needs a bit of love and care, but he's convinced he can fix it up for us, make it something truly ours. What do you say?"

In that moment, as I gazed down at Tony, with the ring shimmering between us, a tumult of emotions swirled within me. I hadn't known him long, yet the depth of my feelings for him was a tangled web I couldn't quite unravel. Was this what love felt like, or was it the allure of an escape? The home he spoke of, a sanctuary from the chaos of my own life—a life marred by the shadows of drinks, drugs, and endless fights—beckoned to me with the promise of peace and belonging.

To be part of his family, to have a place to call my own that wasn't steeped in turmoil, was a dream I scarcely dared to believe could be mine. Tony offered not just a ring, not just a house, but a doorway to a new world, a chance at a life I had longed for but never thought attainable.

With a heart filled with hope and a voice steady with resolve, I found my answer. "Yes," I whispered, the word a key turning in the lock of my future, "I'll marry you."

Months slipped by in a whirlwind of anticipation and hard work, culminating in Tony and I standing in our very own home. Nestled in the heart of a quaint neighbourhood near Prospect Park, our two-bedroom haven represented more than just a place to live; it was a tangible testament to our dreams and determination. Acquiring the mortgage had stretched our finances to their limits, given our modest incomes. However, the house, in dire need of tender loving care, was offered to us at a price we couldn't refuse. It was a project, a challenge, but above all, it was an opportunity.

With sleeves rolled up and spirits high, Tony and his father embarked on a transformative journey, breathing new life into the run down structure. The house slowly shed its worn exterior under their diligent hands, revealing the bones of a home where future memories would be made. As the structural renovations neared completion, we turned our attention to making the space truly ours.

We chose dove grey for the walls, a colour that spoke of serene beginnings and quiet evenings. The plush grey carpet we laid down whispered underfoot, a soft echo of our shared steps towards a future together. Our forays into furniture shopping were filled with laughter and light-hearted debates, ultimately filling our home with sleek, black pieces that stood in bold contrast to the soft walls, a reflection of our combined tastes.

I would often catch myself in moments of quiet reflection, marvelling at the stark contrast between this bright, welcoming space and the bleakness of my past. Memories of the broken-down house on Charles Street, with its empty rooms and cold, bare floorboards, seemed like a distant nightmare. In those dark days, the concept of home felt like an elusive dream, one that flickered and faded with each passing day. Yet, here I was, standing in a reality far removed from those shadows, basking in the warmth of a home that was truly ours.

The journey from that place of hardship to where I stood now, surrounded by the fruits of our labour and the promise of new beginnings, filled me with a profound sense of gratitude. I couldn't help but feel lucky, not just for the bricks and mortar that housed us, but for the love, resilience, and partnership that had built it into a home.

The dawn of our move-in day was marked with a sense of surreal anticipation, a chapter beginning that I had scarcely dared to imagine. Tony, ever my steadfast partner in this journey, drove me to our newly transformed house, a symbol of our shared dreams and endeavours. As I stepped through the door, a wave of emotion washed over me, a mix of disbelief and sheer joy at the realisation of our efforts.

I wandered through each room, a silent observer in a world that felt both familiar and astonishingly new. The beauty of what we had created together was overwhelming, each corner and crevice filled with the tangible evidence of our love and hard work. The kitchen, heart of our home, held a particular charm. I opened the cupboards, one by one, and gently took out mugs and glasses, feeling their weight in my hands. A profound sense of ownership washed over me, a realisation that these simple objects, and indeed this space, were truly mine. "These are mine," I whispered to myself, a mantra affirming my new reality.

The fridge, thoughtfully stocked by Tony's family, stood as a testament to their kindness and support. I stared at the abundance of food, each item a symbol of a life filled with care and community, so starkly different from the scarcity of my past. It was as if I had stepped into a dream, a reality so diametrically opposed to the hardships and deprivation I had known.

Leaving behind 8 Blithe Walk and its shadows of misery, conflict, and unfulfilled hopes was a liberation I had longed for but never fully believed possible. The weight of poverty and disappointment that had characterised my childhood seemed bleak in the light of this new beginning. Here, in this space we had lovingly crafted, was a life that stood in stark contrast to my upbringing, a life filled with promise and potential.

For the first time, I found myself genuinely excited for what lay ahead. The future, once a hazy concept tinged with dread, now beckoned with open arms, inviting me to step into a world of possibilities. The transformation was not just of the house, but of myself; I had stepped out of the shadows of my past and into the light of a future I was eager to embrace.

Chapter Four

The Post Bliss

In the sanctuary of our new home, I found a peace and contentment that had escaped me for years. The stark contrast between this tranquil haven and the turbulent household of my youth was like night and day. I threw myself into making our house a home, dedicating weekends to its upkeep with a zeal that bordered on devout. Each sweep of the broom, each swipe of the cloth was not just about cleanliness; it was a ritual, a celebration of a dream realised. This house was my canvas, and I was determined to maintain its perfection, a physical embodiment of the new life I had so desperately wished for.

Despite the distance from my old life, echoes of its discord found their way to me through my mother's voice. The tales of ongoing arguments, particularly between Ray and Kevin, were reminders of the chaos I had escaped. The intensity of these conflicts seemed only to deepen with time, culminating in a distressing call from my mother. Her voice, thick with tears, conveyed a situation so dire she had felt compelled to involve the police, fearing the worst. The thought of such violence, so close to turning tragic, was a chilling reminder of what I had left behind.

Hearing my mother's plight stirred a tumult of emotions within me. There was a profound sorrow for her continued suffering, a sorrow mingled with a palpable relief that I was no longer a direct witness to the turmoil that plagued my family. This duality of feeling was a heavy burden, reminding me of the bittersweet nature of my escape. While I had found refuge in the arms of a new beginning, those I loved were still caught up in a cycle of strife. The contrast between my current bliss and their ongoing struggle was a stark reminder of the disparities life can present, reinforcing my gratitude for the sanctuary I had found and my resolve to never take it for granted.

Navigating the early stages of our life together, Tony and I encountered the all-too-familiar challenge of balancing our dreams with our financial realities. The mortgage, a tangible commitment to our shared future, loomed large, demanding a level of fiscal discipline we were both unaccustomed to. Despite the daunting task, we persevered, each month's payment a testament to our resilience and determination to build a life on our own terms.

My days were spent immersed in the bustling world of The Prudential, where I diligently pursued my aspiration of becoming a financial advisor. The path was lined with exams and additional learning, each step forward a building block in the foundations of my future career. I found myself assigned to the technical team, a role that involved addressing and resolving customer complaints. I addressed technical inquiries from internal staff, external customers, and associated agencies or organisations related to Life Assurance through both written correspondence and phone communication. It was a position that demanded patience, empathy, and a keen understanding of complex issues—qualities I discovered I possessed in abundance.

Despite a lack of formal achievements in my schooling years, I was pleasantly surprised to find that I thrived in this environment. My success in the role was a stark contrast to my academic past, offering a renewed sense of confidence in my capabilities and potential.

At work, I also found friendship, particularly with a colleague named Kay. Our connection was instant and profound, mirroring the sense of belonging and support I had longed for. Kay, with her shared experiences and understanding, became not just a colleague but a friend, a confidante in the midst of the corporate maze.

This new chapter of my life, marked by professional growth and personal connections, mirrored the stability and focus my mother had found in her own career. It was a revelation to experience first-hand how employment could transcend the mere act of earning a living, providing a sense of purpose and a structure to one's life. The routine and responsibilities of my job became anchors, steadying me amidst the uncertainties of life and reinforcing the value of hard work and ambition. In this newfound stability, I saw not just the blueprint for my career but the foundation of the life Tony and I were determined to build together.

As my twentieth rolled around, mingled with the unpredictable currents of life, an unforeseen twist awaited me, one that I hadn't dared to pencil into my story just yet. The discovery came as silently as a whisper, yet its impact was as thunderous as a storm; my period, a constant since my adolescence, failed to make its appearance. Disbelief shadowed my steps as I sought confirmation through a pregnancy test, which, in its unwavering clarity, declared the beginning of a new chapter: I was pregnant.

The revelation sent shockwaves through my being. Tony and I, we had treaded the path of our relationship with careful steps, enveloped in the warmth of our love yet cautious about the intricacies of our future. Children, a dream we cradled for a day far from now, seemed to have chosen their own timing, paying no heed to our meticulously laid plans. Our savings, while small, had been marked for vows yet to be exchanged, not cradles or diapers.

With a heart heavy yet fluttering with an array of emotions, I sought Tony. His reaction was a mirror of calm waters over a deep, tumultuous sea. Usually an open book, his face concealed his feelings from me. Yet, when he spoke, his words were laced with the weight of reality, a gentle but firm reminder of the battles we were already fighting.

"Donna," he began, his voice a soft echo of our shared concerns, "it's not a good time in our lives to be having a baby. You know it's a struggle just paying the mortgage. How could we afford to bring a child into the world?"

His words, though expected, pierced the bubble of surprise and fear I was encapsulated in. Our love, a beacon in our lives, now faced a storm we hadn't really anticipated and had been careful to avoid. The road ahead, uncertain and daunting, beckoned us to embark on a journey for which we felt unprepared, yet it was one we knew we must undertake, together.

Tony's words, though spoken with a gentle firmness, unleashed a fear within me. In a moment, the present blurred, and I was transported back to a memory etched in the frost of hardship—a memory of my brothers and me, huddled together for warmth in the back of our family car, the cold biting at our skin, a stark reminder of a night when the world had no shelter for us. The sharpness of that memory, against the fragility of our current situation, painted a harrowing picture of potential futures.

The very thought of subjecting my child to the shadows of suffering that once loomed over my childhood filled me with a dread so profound it seemed to echo in the very depths of my soul. The vulnerability of bringing a new life into an uncertain world, possibly to tread the same paths of hardship I had walked, was a risk that loomed large and ominous. It cast a shadow over the initial shock and awe of discovery, morphing into a haunting spectre of potential despair.

And soon, Tony and I found ourselves at a crossroads, faced with a decision that was as heart-wrenching as it was necessary. With a heavy heart, tethered to the ground by the gravity of our reality, I concurred that the most sensible path forward was one of immense emotional and moral complexity—a terminated pregnancy. The decision, though made from a place of love and concern, weighed heavily on us, a testament to the unforeseen trials that love and life often present.

Thus, with a resolve tempered by both love and fear, I took the daunting step of booking an appointment at the clinic. It was a decision shrouded in the bittersweet acknowledgment of what could have been and the sobering acceptance of what needed to be, a poignant reminder of the unpredictable journey of life and the choices we are sometimes compelled to make.

Tony's presence at my side as we journeyed to the clinic was a silent testament to the strength of our bond, a solidarity that neither words nor circumstances could fully articulate. He was there, a pillar of support, as we navigated through the massive sea of decisions that had led us to this point. Throughout the drive, my mind was a battlefield, where echoes of Tony's reasoning clashed with the whispers of my own doubts. I clung to the belief that we were making a prudent choice, a necessary sacrifice to prevent the shadows of my past from darkening the future of another innocent life.

The procedure itself was a blur, thanks to the introduction of general anaesthesia into the world, a temporary escape into oblivion where fears and regrets could not reach. However, the respite was fleeting. Awakening from the operation, I was engulfed by a torrent of emotions, an overwhelming burden of regret that swept away all semblance of certainty and left me adrift in a sea of tears. The realisation hit me with the force of a storm: in my endeavour to shield my future from the spectres of my past, I had allowed those very shadows to dictate a choice that resonated with sorrow rather than relief.

The profound sense of regret that enveloped me was a stark revelation of the intricate ways in which our past experiences weave into the fabric of our present decisions. My childhood, marked by nights of uncertainty and the sting of deprivation, had not been left behind at 8 Blithe Walk as I had fervently hoped. Instead, it had followed me, influencing decisions that bore the weight of permanence. The realisation that my past was still a puppeteer, controlling aspects of my life with strings of fear and trauma, was a bitter pill to swallow.

In that moment of vulnerability, the walls I had built to separate my present from my past crumbled, revealing a truth I had sought to evade: the shadows of 8 Blithe Walk lingered, not just as memories, but as forces that shaped my reality. The decision, made in a crucible of fear and a desire to protect, now stood as a testament to the complex dance between past experiences and present choices. It underscored a poignant lesson about the indelible impact of our histories on our lives and the importance of confronting, rather than fleeing, the ghosts that haunt us.

Returning to everyday life after such a pivotal moment was much like stepping back into a world that had subtly shifted on its axis. Work, once a realm of routine and familiarity, now felt like a landscape marred by invisible fault lines. These fault lines would unexpectedly give way, plunging me into moments of profound grief that surfaced with little warning, leaving me adrift in tears amidst the mundanity of my professional environment. The grief was not just a reflection of loss but a whirlpool of regret over the decision that had seemed so prudent in the shadow of fear, yet now weighed heavily on my heart with the gravity of what could have been.

In this time, solace was elusive, and peace was a horizon that seemed to retreat with every step I took towards it. Yet, amidst the tumult, a flicker of hope began to kindle within the depths of my sorrow—a thought both tender and terrifying in its implications. The idea of having another baby, of giving life to a new hope, became a beacon in the darkness, a distant promise of redemption and renewal. This thought was not about replacing the irreplaceable; rather, it was a yearning for a future where the pain of the past could be woven into the fabric of new beginnings. It offered a vision of a world where the lessons of loss and love could unite with the joy of motherhood, a chance to embrace life's infinite capacity for renewal.

This hope did not erase the pain or negate the complexity of the emotions that enveloped me. It did, however, offer a pathway through the grief, a way to channel the depths of my regret into a forward-looking resolve. It became a quiet affirmation of the resilience of the human spirit, a testament to our ability to find light even in the aftermath of our darkest decisions. The thought of one day holding a child in my arms, not as a replacement but as a testament to the capacity for healing and growth, became a source of comfort and strength, a reminder that even in moments of profound loss, the possibility for new life and love remains.

On an ordinary day, wandering through the heart of town, I found myself inexplicably drawn to the welcoming facade of Mothercare, as if by an invisible thread tugging at the corners of my heart. Stepping inside was like entering a world apart, a sanctuary brimming with the promise of new beginnings. The store, with its aisles lined with tiny garments and the air imbued with the scent of innocence, seemed to echo with the soft gurgles and coos of imagined infants. I found myself gravitating towards the newborn section, my fingers brushing against the soft fabric of baby clothes, each touch a bittersweet caress filled with longing.

As I lingered among the delicate array of babygrows, booties, woolly cardigans, and mittens, a tempting urge took hold of me; an instinctive pull towards motherhood that I hadn't fully allowed myself to feel until that moment. Without conscious thought, I began to fill a basket, selecting items with a tender anticipation that felt both surreal and deeply natural. The colours of lemon yellow became my palette of hope, a neutral palette for the life I yearned to welcome, unmarred by the shadows of past decisions.

The encounter with the sterilising kit around the corner felt like a sign, a practical nudge towards the reality of caring for a baby, and I added it to my basket without hesitation. The weaning kits, with their tiny spoons and cheerful bibs, whispered of future moments filled with laughter and mess, of milestones to be celebrated with joy and pride. Each item I selected was a testament to a future I dared to dream of, a silent vow to a child yet conceived.

As I approached the checkout, a sense of urgency overtook me, a compulsion to solidify this promise to myself before doubt could reclaim its grip. The act of paying for my purchases felt like a rite of passage, an affirmation of my hope and my commitment to a path not yet taken but deeply desired. Walking out of the store, the weight of the shopping bags in my hands was nothing compared to the weight of the longing in my heart—a longing not just for a child, but for the healing and fulfilment that child represented.

In the aftermath of my visit to Mothercare, the reality of my actions began to settle in, leaving me with a mix of confusion and clarity. The proof of my longing, in the form of those two bulging shopping bags, stood as both a ray of hope and a reminder of the journey ahead. It was a journey that would require patience, resilience, and faith in the possibility of new beginnings, a journey towards becoming the mother I aspired to be, fuelled by a love both lost and found.

The clarity of realisation washed over me like a cold shower as I navigated the familiar streets back to our home. The euphoria that had captivated me in the store dissipated, leaving a gnawing anxiety in its wake. What had seemed like a moment of connection to a future dream now felt like a descent into foolishness. Tony's words, a reflection of our shared reality and the careful plans we had laid for our future, echoed in my mind, a stark contrast to the impulsive hope that had led me to purchase those baby items. The fear of his reaction, coupled with the guilt over the financial carelessness, felt like shackles tightening around my heart.

Upon reaching home, the urgency to conceal my actions propelled me upstairs, bypassing the possibility of an immediate confrontation with Tony. The wardrobe, with its hidden compartments behind shoeboxes, became the vault for my secret—a secret that weighed heavily on me, even as I tried to resume normalcy in the aftermath of my actions.

The discovery of the bags by Tony, however, shattered the normalcy I had tried to maintain. His confusion and concern, voiced softly in a question that seemed to echo in the silence of our room, left me grappling for an explanation that eluded my grasp.

"Donna," he said, "why have you bought all this stuff?"

"I just... I don't know," I replied as I couldn't explain it.

"You know this is really weird, don't you?"

I didn't say anything. But deep down, I knew Tony was right.

The reality of my actions was a mirror reflecting back my own internal turmoil. I stood mute, unable to articulate the depth of longing and regret that had driven me to act so out of character.

Tony's words, though not intended to wound, served as a stark reminder of the constant battle between my internal world of grief and the external reality we shared. The inability to return the items, a physical manifestation of my unresolved emotions, meant that they remained hidden, much like the sorrow and longing that continued to dwell within me. Those items, tucked away in the darkness of the wardrobe, became symbols of a loss that was both deeply personal and profoundly isolating.

As the days passed, the hidden baby items served as a constant reminder of the child that could have been, their presence a silent reproach to my aching heart. They stood as guardians of a secret grief, a tangible connection to a dream deferred and a future unclaimed. Like the echoes of the baby's laughter that would never fill our home, they nagged at my conscience, a perpetual whisper of what might have been, and a poignant testament to the complexity of love, loss, and longing.

***

The first cracks in the "perfect" life I had envisioned with Tony gradually began to show, as our paths began to diverge more distinctly with each passing day. The weekends, once a time for shared moments and mutual enjoyment, became a stark illustration of our growing distance. Tony's preference for the camaraderie and laughter found within the walls of the local pub stood in sharp contrast to my own inclination towards the sanctuary of our home. The house, with its familiar corners and comforting silence, offered me a semblance of security and stability in a world that seemed increasingly uncertain. Thus, while Tony sought solace and escape among friends, I found mine in the ritual of cleaning and caring for our space, each polished surface a testament to a longing for control and perfection in the midst of internal chaos.

This divergence in how we sought comfort and connection only served to amplify the distance between us. The more Tony immersed himself in the social warmth of evenings spent away, the colder our shared home felt upon his return. His late nights, sometimes stretching into mornings where the dawn greeted him elsewhere, became a regular pattern. His explanations, though plausible, did little to bridge the emotional gap that yawned ever wider. The phrase, "Oh it was too late so I just crashed at my Mum's," would be repeated every time I'd ask him where he'd been, echoing in the emptiness left by his absence, a refrain that underscored the growing distance in our relationship.

It was not much different even in his presence. A palpable coldness had settled between us, a stark departure from the warmth and intimacy that once defined us. The bed we shared, once a haven of closeness and comfort, now seemed an expanse too vast, with Tony confining himself to his edge, leaving a physical and emotional gulf in the space between us. His diminished affection, both in gesture and in word, mirrored the emotional retreat that had come to characterise our interactions. This growing estrangement, marked by silence and unspoken tensions, became the defining feature of our relationship, a far cry from the shared dreams and aspirations that had once brought us together.

In the silent hours of the night, with Tony lost in slumber, my mind would become a battleground of doubts and fears, echoing the ghosts of past betrayals that had once torn my family apart. The ghost of my father's infidelity, a shadow that had cast a long, dark veil over my childhood, now loomed over my relationship with Tony. The familiar sting of panic, sharp and insidious, wound its way around my heart, compelling me to seek the truth, to dispel the shadows with the light of clarity.

Stealthily, I slipped from the sanctity of our shared bed, driven by a need for answers that gnawed at my peace. The search led me to the tangible evidence of our shared life—Tony's bank statements, a ledger that I hoped would reveal the truth hidden beneath the mundane transactions of our daily existence.

Page after page, I searched for any sign of betrayal: unexplained hotel stays, romantic dinners, or secret gifts. Yet, my meticulous scrutiny revealed nothing out of the ordinary, no clandestine expenditures or hidden affairs. Despite the lack of evidence, the seed of suspicion, once planted, refused to be uprooted, sprouting roots that entwined around my every thought.

Confrontation seemed the only path forward, a desperate plea for truth in the face of mounting paranoia. Tony's denial came swiftly, a mixture of disbelief and hurt colouring his response. His words, meant to reassure, only deepened my turmoil. The life we had built together, in the shared ownership of a home and the pursuit of a collective dream, now felt like a fragile facade, behind which the truth of our disconnect lurked, unseen but palpable.

His accusations of madness, though perhaps born of frustration, echoed ominously in my mind, a reflection of my own growing doubts about my sanity. The paranoia that had taken root was a relentless tormentor, colouring my perception of Tony's every action and absence with the hue of betrayal. The weight of suspicion became a constant companion, overshadowing moments of solitude and turning the spaces between us into chasms of mistrust.

In this existence, where uncertainty had become my constant companion, the once solid foundation of our relationship began to disintegrate, gradually worn away by the unyielding tide of my fears and insecurities. Tony's absences, which I had once accepted because of our differing schedules and commitments, now took on a more sinister tone in my mind. They transformed from simple inconveniences into deliberate acts of abandonment, each departure a tacit confirmation of the darkest, most painful scenarios my imagination could devise.

This shift in perception was not sudden but rather a slow, corrosive process, where doubts grew like weeds, twisting around my thoughts and clouding my judgment. The trust that had once felt as natural as breathing now required a conscious effort to sustain. I found myself scrutinising every word, every gesture, for hidden meanings, interpreting the mundane through a lens distorted by suspicion and fear.

The more I spiralled into this vortex of doubt, the more I realised how these fears were not just about Tony's physical absence but were deeply rooted in a fear of emotional desertion. Each time he left, it wasn't just his presence that I missed but the sense of security and affirmation that came with it. The absence of his voice, his laughter, the reassuring weight of his presence— they left a void that my fears eagerly filled with scenarios of betrayal and rejection.

This was a stark departure from the earlier days of our relationship, where love seemed unshakeable and confidence in each other was unwavering. Now, every unexplained late night, every unanswered call, felt like a brick being removed from the edifice of our love, leaving behind a structure so fragile that even the slightest misunderstanding could threaten its very existence. The challenge I faced was monumental: to confront these fears, to communicate openly with Tony about this growing chasm between us, and to determine whether our relationship could be fortified against the relentless waves of doubt, or if it was doomed to be washed away entirely.

The dread of insanity loomed large, not just as a label wielded in defense by Tony, but as a genuine fear that took root in the fertile ground of my insecurities. The cycle of suspicion and denial, punctuated by moments of desperate clarity, became a prison of my own making, a maze with no clear exit, where the line between reality and imagination blurred, leaving me adrift in a sea of doubt and despair.

One day, when he had once again disappeared, telling me he was at the pub, I had enough. I called my old school friend, Nastashya, saying, "Tony's cheating on me, I'm certain of it. Can you give me a lift to the pub? I need to know what he's up to."

Natashya immediately replied with, "Of course! I'll be round in five minutes."

It wasn't long before I saw the bright lights from her car turning the corner. The drive to the pub with Natashya was a blend of high nerves and the comfort of having an ally in my moment of uncertainty. Her willingness to support me, no questions asked, was a small beacon of warmth in the cold sea of my doubts about Tony.

As we approached our destination, the weight of what I was about to do—confront the reality of my suspicions head-on—made my heart race with anticipation and dread.

Sitting outside the pub, the world seemed to narrow to the frame of the car window, through which I scanned the faces of all who was inside, searching for the one face that would either confirm my fears or offer me relief. Not finding Tony immediately didn't ease my turmoil but rather deepened the pit in my stomach.

Natashya's suggestion to wait, to give the moment a chance to unfold further, was reasonable, yet it did nothing to quell the rising tide of panic within me.

"That's it, he's lying to me," I said.

"Perhaps he's at the bar," suggested Natashya, "We should wait a while."

We sat in the car for a few minutes, and I noticed a strained look on her face.

"What is it? Have you seen something?" I asked, panicked.

"No, no, it's just—I really need the loo!" she replied.

"Well, we can't go inside," I said. "What if Tony's in there with his mates and we suddenly march in? He'll know we've been spying on him."

"Good point," Natashya replied.

Before I could stop her, she was squatting on the floor of the car, peeing into a cup.

"What are you doing?" I asked.

"Well, we can't have our spying mission ruined by my wee!" she retorted, and we both burst into giggles.

The situation, in its entirety, felt like a scene plucked from a far-fetched comedy rather than the reality of two adults trying to navigate the complexities of trust and betrayal. The laughter, a release of built-up tension, also illuminated the absurdity of our predicament. It underscored how far I had strayed from dealing with my concerns in a healthy manner, instead allowing them to lead me into increasingly irrational scenarios.

This moment of ridiculousness, shared with a friend who had shown up to support me in my hour of need, offered a brief respite from the turmoil of my emotions. It reminded me of the importance of perspective, of the need to step back and evaluate the situation not just through the lens of past hurts and fears, but with a view towards understanding and resolution. Yet, even as we shared that brief interval of laughter, the underlying issue remained unresolved, a shadow hanging over the comedic relief of the moment.

Then suddenly, I caught sight of a familiar man, unmistakably clear through the pub's window. It felt like a sharp intake of breath, the kind that precedes a plunge into cold water. The scene before me—him presenting a drink to an attractive woman, their proximity speaking volumes—was the confirmation of my worst fears, a visual echo of the suspicions that had haunted me for months. My laughter faded abruptly and had been replaced by a tightness in my chest, marking the moment my world tilted on its axis.

Natashya had seen what I had and her hand in mine was both a lifeline and a reminder of the immediate choice that lay before me. Her question, laced with concern, mirrored the whirlwind of emotions threatening to overwhelm my composure. My response, a mask of calm, contradicted the turmoil within as I stepped out of the car, fuelled by my need to confront the situation head-on.

"What are you going to do?" she asked in a worried voice.

"Don't worry, I'll handle it," I replied.

Approaching Tony and his companion with a coolness I scarcely felt, I said, "Hello, Tony. Would you like me to buy you a drink too?"

His reaction, a mix of surprise and guilt, was all the acknowledgment I needed of the duplicity that had eroded the foundation of our relationship. My swift departure, an attempt to retain some semblance of dignity, was a silent scream against the injustice of his betrayal.

Natashya's admiration for my outward poise couldn't shield me from the torrent of grief that awaited release. The drive home was a catharsis, each sob a testament to the depth of my pain and betrayal. Tony's actions, a cruel mirror to the past betrayals that had fractured my family, confirmed my deepest fears: history was indeed repeating itself. The parallels were stark—I, too, had lost a child, and now, it seemed, I was on the brink of losing my partner in the same swirling vortex of deceit that had claimed my mother's happiness.

This revelation, this unravelling of my "perfect life", left me teetering on the edge of despair, the shadow of my mother's fate looming large. The fear of succumbing to the same depths of desolation was palpable, threatening to consume my spirit just as it had hers. The realisation that I stood at a crossroads, faced with the choice of succumbing to or overcoming the legacy of loss and abandonment that had haunted my family, was both daunting and clarifying.

In this moment of profound vulnerability, the journey ahead was uncertain, yet it beckoned with the promise of self-discovery and renewal. The pain of the present, while overwhelming, also offered an opportunity to forge a path defined not by the echoes of the past but by the strength found in facing and overcoming adversity.

Chapter Five

The Aftermath

Late one afternoon, as the golden hues of sunlight filtered through the half-drawn blinds, casting a warm but sombre glow across the room that on some days, I was lying on the sofa, lost in a haze of fatigue and heartache.

The world outside seemed distant, muffled by the thick veil of depression that had enveloped me since the tumultuous end of my relationship with Tony. It was during these months of solitude, battling the relentless grip of glandular fever, that my life had shrunk to the confines of my living room. Work, meals, even the simple act of climbing the stairs and onto my bed had become insurmountable tasks. My existence had been reduced to a life where days melded into nights in an indistinguishable blur, and my only solace was the cocoon of blankets and the steady hum of the outside world that I tried desperately to ignore.

The sudden, insistent knock at the door that afternoon pierced my bubble of isolation like a needle through fabric. A part of me instinctively knew it was someone from my family who, sensing my struggle, had been watching over me with worried eyes in my otherwise quiet life. The breakup with Tony had been a catalyst, not just for the fever that ravaged my body, but for the outpouring of love and worry from my family, who felt my pain as if it was their own, offering support, a kind word or maybe even a home-cooked meal.

Dragging myself up with an effort that felt monumental, I made my way to the door. It creaked open to reveal Mark, my brother whose presence always seemed to carry a light with it. The look on his face was enough to tell me that my attempts to appear "fine" were fooling no one. His eyes, usually so full of joy and laughter, were clouded with worry.

"Donna, you need to eat more," he said, his tone firm but caring. "Look at you, you've lost so much weight." He wasn't wrong. I had always been on the slender side, but now my clothes hung loosely, and my face had lost its healthy glow. The energy to even think about food shopping, let alone actually do it, had deserted me weeks ago. Tony's mother had taken up the mantle, ensuring that groceries found their way to my doorstep, a bridge of compassion that remained steadfast even as the ties between her son and me had been severed. It was a kindness I hadn't expected, a small lifeline in a sea of overwhelming lethargy and sadness.

Mark's visit, his straightforward concern, was a reminder of the network of care that surrounded me, even when I felt most alone. It was easy to forget, in the midst of illness and heartbreak, that there were people ready and willing to help, to pull me back from the brink. With Mark standing in my doorway, I was reminded that it was these threads that held the promise of healing, woven with the care of those who refused to let me face my darkest hours alone.

"Mum's been ringing you, but you don't answer the phone," said my brother. "What's going on?"

His eyes, a mirror to the worry that crept into his voice, searched mine for an answer I felt unequipped to provide. In the depths of my being, a turmoil churned, its roots tangled in a complex web of emotions and circumstances that I struggled to unravel. The illness that had stealthily woven its shadows around my days was but a fragment of the weight I bore. Since Tony made the decision to move back into his parent's house with his new girlfriend, I found myself receding further into the shadows of my own existence. A profound disinterest in the world around me had taken hold, a familiar darkness that I recognised from the lost years of my youth. Back then, the cloak of my isolation was a mystery. Yet, as the days melded into a monochrome blur, the realisation dawned upon me: depression, a silent thief of joy, had once again crept into my life.

The unravelling had begun with Tony's betrayal, a wound that time seemed incapable of healing. His return, after a few days of the confrontation at the pub, cloaked in apologies and woven with excuses, failed to mend the gap his absence had created. My resolve to sever the ties that bound us was ironclad, fortified by the knowledge that the shards of trust shattered between us could never be pieced back together. Yet, the thought of abandoning Albany Road, the sanctuary that had cradled my dreams of a serene existence, was a prospect too harrowing to entertain. It was the first place I had truly called home, a haven far removed from the tumultuous storms of 8 Blithe Walk.

The idea of loosening my grip on this fragment of peace was unbearable. I yearned to sever Tony's claim on this home, to buy him out so I could claim it as my own. Yet he stood opposed, an immovable force against my desires. Our interactions, though initially cloaked in the guise of civility, inevitably descended into chaos, a tempest of words and emotions that left us both frayed. With each encounter, the sense of being trapped in an endless cycle of conflict and despair deepened, a noose tightening around the remnants of my hope.

In the quiet aftermath of my prolonged absence from work, the understanding initially shown by my employers began to wane, subtly replaced by concern. It wasn't long before my boss, with a tone of gentle insistence, made a suggestion over the phone that perhaps it was time for me to seek medical advice, hinting at the possibility of medication. This nudge, albeit faint, was enough to spark a flicker of resolve within me, and I found myself muster the strength to attend a doctor's appointment. There, after a conversation that seemed both fleeting and eternal, I was prescribed Prozac, a name I'd heard whispered in corridors but never imagined would be part of my narrative.

Gradually, the fog began to lift just enough for me to envisage a return to work. Yet, each day felt Herculean in its demand as I trudged through the motions, my evenings collapsing into a routine of sheer exhaustion: home, eat, and then a descent into sleep's forgetful embrace. My existence became a monotonous cycle, where the only semblance of relief was found in the smoke of cigarettes, inhaled with a desperation that mirrored my brother Mark's own struggles. The habit had ensnared me completely, becoming my companion in the early hours, my solace at noon, and my last encounter before the night.

Amidst this personal turmoil, a piercing blow came with the news of Tony's girlfriend's pregnancy. There were moments when the reality of it confronted me viscerally, as I caught glimpses of her beside him in his car, her pregnancy unmistakably evident. Each sighting was a sharp reminder of the path not taken; the future I had aborted alongside my unborn child. The baby clothes, purchased in a haze of sorrow, remained untouched, hidden in the depths of my wardrobe—a testament to a dream that had turned to dust.

The house that once symbolised a fresh start, painstakingly decorated by Tony and me in brighter days, now stood as a mausoleum of shattered dreams. It was in this space that we had envisioned a life free from the shadows of familial strife, a sanctuary of our own making. Yet, as I moved through its rooms, I was haunted by the ghost of what could have been, each corner a cruel reminder of a promise unfulfilled. The vibrant hopes and dreams that once filled these walls now lay as relics of a life that had quietly slipped away, leaving behind a silence too profound to ignore.

The days melded into an unending loop of monotony and routine, punctuated only by the demands of a job that felt increasingly impossible, restless nights haunted by dreams unremembered, and clashes with Tony that left the air heavier and my heart a little more frayed. Amidst all this, I existed, a shadow of myself, merely surviving rather than living.

My mother would often make her sporadic visits, each time attempting to pierce the gloom that clung to me like a second skin. Despite the demands of her job as a supervisor at the local convenience store, she carved out moments to bring a semblance of light into my days. Yet, with each visit, her worry for me deepened, her brow furrowing a little more, her smiles a bit more strained.

Determined to wrench me away from my miserable state, she took a bold step one day. The phone call that would set her plan into motion came unexpectedly.

"Donna," she declared with a resolve that encouraged no argument, "I've arranged a date for you. This Friday night, we're going out for dinner with a young man from near the shop. His name's Hassan, he's gorgeous—and he's a doctor!" Her voice was alight with excitement, a stark contrast to the weariness that seemed my constant companion.

Her enthusiasm, however palpable, failed to ignite any spark of interest within me. The prospect of social interaction, let alone a date, felt as daunting as scaling a mountain. "I'm just too tired, Mum. I wouldn't be good company," I protested, my voice a whisper of defeat.

Undeterred, she responded, "Well, if you don't like the look of him, you can always leave. But dinner's already booked! See you on Friday." The line went dead before I could muster any further objection.

I hung up the phone, a sigh escaping me. Poor Mum. Her intentions were as pure as they were transparent, seeking to lift me from the mess of my existence with a gesture so full of hope it ached. Yet, a thought lingered, unwanted and heavy: What man would desire the company of a woman so ensnared by her past, a perpetual smoker shrouded in the remnants of a life shared with another?

As the days slowly wound their way to Friday, a sense of reluctance cloaked me, heavier than the autumn air. Yet, bound by a mixture of duty and a faint, inexplicable curiosity, I found myself navigating the familiar streets to our chosen meeting place: a cosy pub that seemed to promise warmth and laughter within its aged walls. The moment I stepped inside, the sight that greeted me was unexpected, disarming even. There stood Mum, her presence a familiar comfort, but it was the man beside her who captured my immediate attention. Tall and striking, with an aura of gentle confidence, Hassan was a vision of contrasts compared to the figures from my past. His dark, wavy hair framed a face that bore the undeniable marks of his Palestinian heritage, each feature sculpted as though with careful thought. There was an undeniable "wow" factor about him, a charisma that seemed to emanate in waves. Yet, as fate would have it, my heart was a fortress that night, impervious to the charms that might have once stirred it.

We settled into our seats, the table on a small island in the pub. Mum, ever the effervescent spirit, filled the space between us with her lively chatter, weaving her maternal magic in an attempt to bridge any gaps that might linger in the air. Hassan, to his credit, engaged with her with a grace that was both endearing and remarkable. There was a warmth in his demeanour, a respectful amusement that never veered into condescension. Despite the oddity of our gathering—a date orchestrated by a mother for her dispirited daughter—Hassan navigated the evening with an ease that bordered on the extraordinary. His ability to transform what could easily have been an awkward assembly into an occasion that felt almost natural was not lost on me. Amidst the soft glow of the pub lights and the gentle murmur of conversations around us, I found myself reluctantly drawn in, impressed by the man who had managed to make an unlikely scenario seem almost right.

As the evening unfolded, the layers of Hassan's story were peeled away, revealing not the medical practitioner my mother had envisioned, but a scholar with a doctorate—a twist that only added to the intrigue of his character. His journey had brought him from the academic corridors of Reading to the bustling heart of London, where he now imparted his knowledge at City University. This revelation did nothing to diminish his appeal; if anything, it painted him in a more profound light. Despite the lofty realms of engineering and academia he navigated, Hassan was refreshingly grounded. His humour, both playful and intelligent, sparkled through the conversation, creating a bridge between him and my ever-joyful mother. Their rapport was undeniable, a blend of wit and laughter that seemed to fill the spaces around us with a lightness I longed to grasp.

Yet, for all the warmth that flickered at our table, I remained adrift, a mere witness of their lively exchange. The weight of my own shadows—fatigue and a relentless depression—anchored me firmly outside the circle of their companionship. The dialogue, rich with laughter and insights, seemed to meander through a world I could barely touch, its threads slipping through my fingers like mist. In that moment, I was convinced of my own invisibility, certain that my presence was as negligible as my readiness for any venture into the realm of romance.

The surprise that awaited me the following week was as unexpected as a bolt of sunlight through storm clouds. Hassan's voice, emerging from the other end of a phone call, carried with it an invitation that halted me in my tracks—an offer to dine once more.

"This time, without your Mum—much as I love her!" he teased, his quip carrying a lightness that momentarily lifted the heaviness from my shoulders.

His words were laced with humour and a hint of warmth that seemed to challenge the cold resignation I had wrapped around myself. The shock of his call, the realisation that he saw beyond the fog that I felt enveloped me, ignited a flicker of something unexpected, perhaps you could even call it a sliver of hope. Could it be that under the skeleton of my existence, there remained a glimmer of possibility for me to find love again? While the very idea of love seemed as foreign as it did frightening, Hassan's invitation held a promise that there may still be chance for me to step beyond the shadows into the light.

The unexpected flutter of flattery was potent enough to momentarily eclipse my reservations, compelling a "yes" from lips that had grown accustomed to saying no to life. Yet, as the connection was severed and the phone returned to its silent vigil, the shadows that had momentarily receded surged back with renewed vigour. The haunting phantom of my past experiences, particularly the deep scars left by Tony's betrayal, cast a long, chilling shadow over the fragile spark of optimism that Hassan's interest had kindled.

Tony's actions had not merely fractured my trust in others; they had shattered the very foundation of my self-esteem and my capacity to envision a future tinted with the hues of joy and fulfilment. The betrayal had been a corrosive acid, eating away at the ties that bound me to hope, leaving behind a husk resigned to a life diminished, where dreams were relics of a naive past self. In the aftermath, I had constructed a sanctuary of sorts within the confines of my living room, my sofa becoming both shield and prison, safeguarding the remnants of stability I clung to with a desperation that was as much about fear as it was about preservation.

The prospect of venturing beyond this self-imposed exile, of allowing someone new to glimpse the vulnerabilities and shadows that I harboured, felt akin to stepping out onto a precipice with no assurance of solid ground beneath my feet.

The very idea of intertwining my life with another's, of daring to believe that happiness could be more than a fleeting visitor in my world, seemed an affront to the lessons etched into my heart by disappointment and despair. I was ensnared in a limbo of my own making, caught between the faint glimmer of possibility that Hassan represented and the deep-seated conviction that my place was one of isolation, tethered to the last vestiges of an existence that, while barren, promised the safety of the known.

In this twilight of my spirit, where light and shadow warred with silent ferocity, the path forward was obscured. The invitation to dinner, a simple gesture under ordinary circumstances, loomed as a monumental decision—a crossroads where the choice lay not just in accepting or declining an offer of companionship, but in confronting the very essence of what I believed about myself and the potential for healing and growth beyond the ruins of my past.

On that particular evening, as the twilight embraced London, there was a knock at my door that seemed to echo with a promise. Standing there, framed by the soft glow of the hallway light, was Hassan, every bit the embodiment of the hope I dared not fully grasp. In his hands, he bore the timeless tokens of affection: a bouquet of flowers, vibrant and fragrant, alongside a box of chocolates, their sweetness a metaphor for the possibilities that lay before us. With a smile that seemed to banish the shadows, he ushered me into the night, towards an Italian oasis nestled in the heart of west London. There, amidst the rustic charm and the soft serenade of a distant melody, we found ourselves lost in a world apart, the candlelight between us casting a glow that seemed to soften the edges of reality.

As the evening progressed, a familiar adversary whispered doubts and insecurities, painting me as unworthy of the man who sat across from me. His world, rich in academia and intellectual pursuits, seemed a realm apart from mine, despite my own strides into a career that bore the impressive title of "Technical

Advisor" at The Prudential. Yet, in the face of my internal tumult, Hassan remained unfazed. His demeanour lacked any hint of condescension; instead, he possessed an innate ability to bridge the gap of our experiences, drawing me out into laughter and conversation with an ease that felt both exhilarating and disarming. Here was a man of maturity and intellect, a stark contrast to the shadows of my past, embodying a solidity and reliability I had long yearned for but scarcely believed I deserved.

Despite the warmth of connection and the genuine enjoyment that flickered to life in those moments, the depression clung to me with tenacious fingers. It was an unseen anchor that tethered me to a familiar refuge of isolation, even as the currents of potential joy and companionship beckoned. My interactions with Hassan became a dance of advance and retreat, a cycle where moments of closeness were invariably followed by periods of withdrawal. Each encounter with him represented a step towards something beautiful and rare, yet the gravity of my own internal struggles invariably pulled me back, enforcing a solitude that was both sanctuary and prison.

This pattern of connection and withdrawal, of reaching towards the light only to recoil into the shadows, underscored a tumultuous journey. It was a reflection of the battle within—a struggle between the desire for love and happiness, and the chains of past pain and present fears. My heart, caught in this ebb and flow, yearned to break free from the cycle, to embrace the promise of something new and healing with Hassan. Yet, the road to such a destination was fraught with the debris of old wounds and the ever-present shadow of doubt, making each step forward a testament to both vulnerability and courage.

The journey with Hassan, marked by gradual openings and cautious optimism, took an unexpected turn with the arrival of a revelation that had the potential to challenge the equilibrium we had painstakingly established. The nature of such bombshells is their capacity to unsettle, to unearth questions and fears that might have lain dormant, and to test the foundations upon which connections are built.

In relationships, particularly those still in their formative stages like ours was, the introduction of unforeseen complications or revelations can act as both a crucible and a catalyst. The resilience of the bond between the individuals involved, the depth of their commitment to one another, and their capacity for understanding and empathy are put to the test.

The true mettle of a relationship is often revealed in how both individuals navigate these choppy waters—whether they choose to retreat to the safety of their respective shores or find a way to bridge the divide with honesty, openness, and a willingness to face the challenges together. The ability to weather such storms, to emerge on the other side with a bond that is, if not unscathed, then at least strengthened by the trial, speaks volumes about the potential longevity and resilience of the relationship.

In the context of my evolving relationship with Hassan, the revelation that he had a nine-year-old daughter named Leila presented an opportunity for us to take our relationship to the next emotional level and become even closer.

It marked a moment of profound significance, a tender juncture where the personal met the parental, bridging worlds in a way that felt both intimate and expansive. The anticipation of meeting her carried a weight of its own, laden with the potential to redefine the contours of my connection with Hassan. His desire for me to meet his daughter, expressed with a sincerity that touched something deep within me, emphasised the depth of his trust and the seriousness with which he regarded our relationship.

The day we set out to Heathrow was etched with a sense of momentousness, the journey more than mere transit; it was a pilgrimage towards a new chapter. The moment Leila stepped into view, any reservations I might have harboured were swept away by the immediate enchantment of her presence. She was a striking blend of her heritage—half Palestinian, with the nuanced beauty of her father's lineage, a quarter Irish, and a quarter English, her unique blend manifesting in striking blue-green eyes that seemed to capture the very essence of the seas and skies, set against the warmth of her tanned skin and the dark cascade of her hair. In her, I saw the embodiment of worlds coming together, a living testament to the beauty of blended cultures and histories.

Our venture into the heart of town the following day was an exercise in bonding, a delightful exploration of the simple joys that shopping and shared experiences can bring. The selection of a trendy new doll for Leila, an act so ordinary yet imbued with significance, became a symbol of acceptance and connection. Hassan's playful disapproval, coupled with the warmth in his eyes, spoke volumes of the bond forming between us, a bond that extended beyond the confines of romantic involvement to touch upon the realms of family and shared future possibilities.

In the laughter and light of that day, in the easy rapport that sprung up between Leila and me, there was a glimpse of something profound and potentially transformative. The significance of their acceptance, of the open-hearted embrace of this new dynamic, was not lost on me. It was a validation, a silent affirmation from Hassan that my place in his life was not just as a partner but as a potential figure of significance in Leila's life as well. This unfolding relationship, with its delicate new dimensions, offered a vision of a future I had scarcely dared to contemplate; a future where love, trust, and shared experiences might weave a fabric strong enough to support the weight of past sorrows and present fears.

The transformation in my life—from the shadows of a not-so-great past to the dawn of a hopeful future—was nothing short of miraculous. The presence of Hassan and, by extension, Leila, in my life had gently coaxed my heart open, nurturing within me the blossoming of something I had long resigned myself to live without: a sense of belonging, of family, that was both loving and serene. This newfound connection, so starkly different from the fraught ties of my childhood, offered a glimpse into a world I had yearned for but scarcely believed possible.

When Leila left to go back to Ireland, rather than leaving a void, it seemed to solidify the bond between Hassan and me, drawing us closer in a shared vision of the future. The seeds of hope for a loving family life, once buried deep beneath layers of doubt and hurt, began to sprout with renewed vigour. It was in this fertile ground of renewed trust and affection that Hassan chose to propose, and without a shred of the hesitation that once would have clouded such a moment, I accepted. The certainty that filled me was a testament to the depth of our connection, a stark contrast to the murky waters of my past entanglements.

The practicalities of merging our lives together, while daunting, were steps I approached with a sense of clarity and purpose. The decision to let Tony buy me out of our shared property was not just a financial transaction; it was a symbolic release from a chapter of my life that was ready to be closed, a final cutting of ties that freed me to fully embrace the future that lay ahead with Hassan. The modest sum I would receive, far from being just a financial cushion, represented the means to craft a celebration of our union—a wedding that would signify not just the joining of two lives but the culmination of a journey from despair to hope.

Hassan's living situation in Reading, marked by discord with his flatmates, prompted a decision to seek temporary refuge with Mum as we navigated the early stages of our marriage and the search for a home of our own. The irony of returning to the very house I had once been so eager to escape was not lost on me. Yet, the circumstances of my return were imbued with a different essence. It was a testament to the transformative power of love and the prospect of a new beginning. This was not a retreat to old patterns, but a strategic step towards the future we were eager to build together.

In this pivotal chapter of my existence, each decision I made, every path I chose, carried with it a deep sense of deliberation and purpose, as if I were carefully placing each thread into the intricate tapestry of a future I was meticulously crafting. The very prospect of moving back, even for a short period, into an environment laden with difficult memories, was met with a resilience that sprang from an awareness that this was merely a transient chapter in the larger narrative of our intertwined dreams and aspirations.

This period of transition was buoyed by the unwavering support and understanding of my mother, whose strength and wisdom were my anchors in turbulent seas. The palpable anticipation of building a life with Hassan added layers of excitement and promise to my days, transforming mundane moments into stepping stones towards our shared future. The vision of a life characterised by love, mutual respect, and shared goals shone brightly ahead, serving as a guiding light as I navigated the complexities of healing and renewal.

This was more than a mere sequence of events; it was a profound journey of healing, a deliberate process of opening my heart to love and endless possibilities, and a bold step into a future that, for the first time in a significant while, appeared not only hopeful but distinctly attainable. Every moment of uncertainty, every challenge faced, was imbued with a sense of purpose and direction, knowing that each step taken was a move towards a life we dreamt of and believed in. It was a time of transformation where the past, with all its trials and tribulations, was not a chain holding me back but a lesson propelling me forward towards a future filled with promise and the warmth of shared dreams.

Chapter Six

The Wedding

June 14, 2003, the happiest day of my life, dawned as a day etched with the promise of new beginnings and the culmination of a journey from shadows into light. The meticulous planning of the event reflected not just the depth of our commitment to each other but also the shared joy and anticipation of weaving our lives together. The theme of the day was a symphony of lilac, a hue that painted every detail with the brush of our chosen harmony—from the bouquet I held in my trembling hands to the delicate accents on my dress and the silk of Hassan's tie. It was a visual testament to our story, a palette chosen for its tranquillity and its subtle echo of the dreams we were creating together.

My wedding gown, a strapless creation that combined elegance with a whisper of tradition, was the single most extravagant purchase I had ever made. Yet, in every fibre of its being, it felt like a worthy investment; a tangible representation of the importance of this day. Adorned with a tiara, a veil as white as the promises we were set to exchange, and a diamante choker that caught the light with every movement, I felt transformed, not just in appearance but in spirit. The arrival of the limousine was a moment of surreal beauty, a chariot for the journey ahead, with Leila, my cherished bridesmaid, sharing in the joy and dressed in a lilac frock that mirrored the day's theme. Her excitement added a layer of innocence and wonder to the proceedings.

As I stole a glance at Hassan, clad in his navy suit, the magnitude of the moment settled over me. The man who stood before me, ready to embark on this shared journey, was a far cry from the future I had once envisioned with someone else. In Hassan, I found not just a partner, but a beacon of hope, understanding, and unwavering support—a realisation that really emphasised on the serendipity of our union.

Our marriage, formalised in the understated yet profound setting of a registry office, was only the beginning. To honour my long-held dream of a white wedding, we sought the blessings of a church ceremony, complete with the solemnity of a bible reading and the soul-stirring notes of "Amazing Grace" filling the air. The transition to the Hillingdon Hotel for the reception was a seamless continuation of the celebration—a gathering imbued with love, laughter, and the shared happiness of friends and family. The décor, a blend of white and lilac, mirrored the thematic essence of our union, with candles casting a soft glow over the tables and lilac envelopes hinting at the thoughtful favours within. The crowning glory was the wedding cake, adorned with decorations meticulously crafted by Mum, a labour of love that added a deeply personal touch to the festivities.

As I stood amidst the perfection of that day, surrounded by the tangible expressions of love and commitment, the realisation dawned that every step taken, every choice made, had led me to this moment of unbridled joy. The path that had once seemed fraught with uncertainty had unfolded into a journey of love, healing, and the discovery of a shared future that was both a dream realised and a testament to the unexpected gifts that life can offer. June 14, 2003, was not just the happiest day of my life; it was the beginning of a new chapter, rich with the potential for love, growth, and the creation of memories to cherish for a lifetime.

Despite the meticulous planning and the fairy-tale ambiance of the day, the reception was not without its moments of discord, courtesy of Ray's predictable drunken shenanigans. His appearance, donned in an England football shirt, clashed starkly with the carefully curated elegance of the occasion. His attempt to mingle, a staggering dance of miscommunication exacerbated by his thick Geordie accent and the fog of alcohol, presented a scene that was as amusing as it was cringe-worthy.

Meanwhile, Kevin's absence was noted with a mix of disappointment and resignation. His battle with substances had rendered him a ghost in the celebration, missing from the ceremony and the lasting memories captured in photographs. Yet, these episodes, rather than taking away from the joy of the day, emphasised a profound shift in perspective. The decision to not let these moments overshadow the significance of the occasion was a testament to the resilience and growth that had marked my journey to this point. This day was a celebration of love, hope, and the beauty of new beginnings, undimmed by the shadows of past challenges.

The night spent at the hotel was a continuation of the dream, a bubble of happiness with Leila settled safely nearby, a picture-perfect idea of the new family we were becoming. The morning brought with it a poignant transition from celebration to reflection as Hassan accompanied Leila to the airport, a farewell that was both an end and a beginning.

Meanwhile, the gesture of bringing the wedding flowers to Nan and Grandad's grave, accompanied by Mum and Mark, was a bridge between past and present, a tribute to the roots from which my life had grown. It was a moment of quiet homage; a wish whispered to the breeze that my Nan could have witnessed the transformation of her granddaughter's life. The vision of marrying a man as noble and accomplished as Hassan, who carried the title of "Dr." before his name, was something I knew would have filled her with pride and joy.

This act of remembering and honouring where I came from, even as I stepped boldly into a new chapter of my life, was a powerful affirmation of the journey I had undertaken. It was a recognition that while the past may shape us, it does not define us. The beauty of life lies in our ability to rise, to evolve, and to find happiness and fulfilment in the face of adversity. My wedding day, and the quiet reflection that followed, was a celebration not just of love and union, but also of personal triumph, of the capacity to dream and to realise those dreams against all odds. It was a declaration that from the ashes of a troubled past, a future filled with love, hope, and beauty could indeed flourish.

The next day, I embarked on our honeymoon to Cuba with Mum and Hassan. Including my Mum on this journey was a gesture steeped in gratitude and love, a reflection of the unconventional yet profound bond that had been the catalyst for Hassan and me coming together. Her matchmaking efforts, driven by a mother's intuition and desire for her daughter's happiness, had blossomed into a love story that warranted celebration beyond the boundaries of tradition. Her efforts deserved a reward, and during the honeymoon, I made sure to give her a once-in-a-lifetime moment by swimming with the dolphins together.

Despite the unique dynamics of my family, marked by the absence of a father figure that could have led to a lack of direction, Hassan seamlessly integrated with my relatives, understanding and accepting the complexities of my family background. This understanding fostered a bond not only between us but also extended to my family members, illustrating the depth of his empathy and the strength of our connection.

Hassan's family, residing far from us in Amman, Jordan, expressed their happiness for both of us, extending a warm welcome that transcended geographical distances and cultural differences. Their acceptance and kindness were heart-warming, making me feel a valued part of Hassan's family despite the physical miles that separated us.

Following our marriage, we took the opportunity to visit my in-laws in Jordan, a trip that was significant in bridging the gap between our families and cultures. During this visit, we shared with Hassan's parents a copy of our wedding video and photo album, tangible memories of our special day. This gesture was more than just a sharing of happy moments; it was a symbol of the merging of our lives and families, fostering a connection and understanding that would lay the foundation for our future together. The warm reception and genuine happiness from Hassan's family underscored the universal language of love and acceptance, reinforcing the bonds between us despite the physical and cultural distances.

Returning to 8 Blithe Walk after the idyllic interlude in Cuba presented a stark contrast to the life Hassan and I had begun to dream of together. The space, now devoid of Kevin's presence, offered a semblance of tranquillity, a canvas on which we hoped to paint the early days of our married life. Yet, the reality of our situation, cramped within the confines of what was essentially a makeshift home, was a constant reminder of the dreams and aspirations that lay just beyond our grasp. With Hassan embarking on the daily commute to London and myself immersed in the pursuit of further qualifications, our lives became a blur of activity, with precious little time spent within the walls of 8 Blithe Walk. Our focus was singular: to lay the foundations for our future, to secure a space that was truly our own.

However, as the days unfolded, a subtle disquiet began to pierce the fabric of our existence. Hassan, my partner, whose resilience and determination had always been a source of inspiration, began to exhibit signs of an internal struggle that neither of us fully understood. The shadow of his past dispute with his former employers, despite its resolution in his favour, loomed large, a phantom that haunted his thoughts and conversations with a persistence that was both alarming and heart-breaking.

The initial quirks, easily dismissed as eccentricities or the simple forgetfulness that afflicts us all at times, gradually evolved into unmistakable signs of a deeper issue. The transformation from the man I knew, capable and confident, to someone who struggled with the basics of daily life, was both profound and distressing. His misadventures—returning from simple errands with unexpected items, wearing mismatched shoes, and losing track of time and place—were initially met with humour. Yet, as these incidents became more frequent and more pronounced, the laughter died in our throats, replaced by a growing sense of fear and confusion.

The possibility that the stress and trauma of his tribunal experience might be manifesting in such a tangible and destructive way was a thought too terrifying to contemplate. Yet, I couldn't help but wonder if the chaos of our current living situation, a far cry from the stability we both craved, was contributing to his decline. The question of whether these were signs of a breakdown or something even more serious loomed large, casting a shadow over the future we had envisioned together.

Faced with this crisis, the path forward was unclear, but the necessity of seeking help was undeniable. The man I loved, the partner with whom I had vowed to share my life, was slipping away, consumed by a battle that neither of us fully understood. It was a moment that called for courage, for action, and for the strength to support Hassan through the storm, to navigate the uncertain waters ahead with the hope of finding a way back to each other and to the future we had dreamed of.

We decided to see the GP immediately. The journey to the GP's office was fraught with a mix of apprehension and hope, my heart heavy with the weight of unspoken fears. As I poured out my concerns to the doctor, his measured inquiries about

Hassan's recent history hinted at the seriousness of the situation. The mention of head injuries, a potential trigger for cognitive decline, momentarily sparked a flicker of relief before the reality of our circumstances set in once more.

When we confirmed that Hassan had not suffered any recent head injuries, the GP's swift referral to the Neurology Department at the Royal Berkshire Hospital sent a shiver down my spine. The urgency of his actions underscored the gravity of our situation, casting a shadow over our hopes for a simple explanation or a quick remedy.

The journey to the Royal Berkshire Hospital, marked by a mix of dread and desperate hope, culminated in a moment that would forever alter the course of our lives. Sitting in the sterile calm of the waiting room, the difference between Hassan's detached demeanour and the trembling fear within me seemed to deepen with each passing minute. His disconnection, a protective veil against the unknown, contrasted sharply with the storm of emotions raging within me as we awaited our turn to see the neurologist.

The moment we were ushered into the consulting room, the air heavy with anticipation, the neurologist's expression bore the weight of the news before a word was spoken. The diagnosis of early onset Alzheimer's, delivered with a gravity and compassion that emphasised the severity of the situation, landed like a blow. The term "early onset" echoed ominously, a stark reminder of the cruel incongruity of such a condition afflicting someone of Hassan's age, vitality, and promise.

The revelation shattered the envisioned future that had once seemed so bright and attainable. Plans for a home, a family, and decades of shared experiences were suddenly overshadowed by the ghost of a disease more commonly associated with the elderly. The diagnosis seemed to mock our hopes and dreams, casting them into the realm of the unattainable, transforming them into ghosts of what might have been.

Hassan's reaction, or the lack thereof, to the devastating news only intensified the sense of isolation and despair. His apparent detachment, whether a symptom of the disease or a defense mechanism against the unimaginable, felt like an impossible barrier in a moment when connection and understanding were most needed.

The neurologist's words, though intended to inform and guide us through the next steps, faded into a blur of incomprehension. The mention of further tests, potential treatments, and the reality of living with Alzheimer's became background noise to the deafening silence that the words "early onset Alzheimer's" had wrought. In that instant, the future we had so eagerly anticipated seemed to crumble, leaving in its wake a landscape of uncertainty, fear, and grief.

The diagnosis of early onset Alzheimer's was not just a medical condition; it was a life-altering reality that challenged the very essence of our shared dreams and aspirations. It marked the beginning of a journey fraught with challenges, requiring strength, resilience, and an unwavering commitment to navigate the uncharted waters ahead. As we left the consulting room, the weight of our new reality settled upon us, a stark reminder of the fragility of life and the unpredictability of fate. Yet, within this whirlwind of emotion, the resolve to face the future together, to support and love each other through the coming trials, began to take root, a beacon of hope amidst the storm.

As we descended the steps of the hospital, the weight of the diagnosis hung heavy in the air, casting a pall over our every step. Tears blurred my vision, a silent testament to the anguish that threatened to engulf me, yet Hassan's seemingly indifferent question about dinner pierced through the fog of despair. It was a stark reminder of the disconnect between our realities, a jarring juxtaposition of the mundane and the monumental.

In that moment, the enormity of our situation crashed over

me like a tidal wave, drowning out any semblance of hope or optimism. The dreams we had dared to nurture, the fragile threads of happiness we had woven together, all seemed to unravel before my eyes. It was as though life itself had conspired against us, snatching away the promise of a future we had dared to envision.

The nightmare of reality closed in around me, suffocating any remnants of faith or trust I had dared to harbour. The tendrils of despair tightened their grip, threatening to pull me under, leaving me gasping for air in a sea of uncertainty and fear. How could we ever escape the suffocating confines of 8 Blithe Walk now, with the weight of Hassan's illness bearing down upon us like an anchor?

The prospect of becoming Hassan's full-time carer loomed ominously on the horizon, a burden too heavy to bear yet impossible to ignore. The road ahead stretched out before us, fraught with obstacles and challenges that seemed insurmountable. And yet, amidst the darkness that threatened to consume us, there flickered a glimmer of determination—a stubborn refusal to surrender to despair.

Though the future appeared bleak and uncertain, we refused to be defined by the limitations imposed upon us. Together, we would face the trials that lay ahead, drawing strength from each other in the face of adversity. For even in the darkest of moments, there remained a sliver of hope—a beacon of light that refused to be extinguished, guiding us forward through the storm.

Norma, Donna's mother.

Donna's grandad Norman, who committed suicide.

77

Donna's nan, grandad & mother - Ivy, Norman & Norma.

Donna with her 3 brothers Mark, Garry & Kevin.

Mother and children in search for home

A MOTHER-OF-FOUR was given a temporary reprieve by Reading Council last night after earlier fears that she was to be made homeless.

Mrs Norma Taylor and her four children were earlier told to leave a council flat where they had been staying illegally.

They feared they would have to leave last night and go on a lonely drive through the town to find a new home.

Mrs Taylor and her children were staying with her mother, Mrs Ivy Wilkinson, without Reading's housing department's knowledge.

But last night the social services department found Mrs Taylor and her children temporary accommodation in a bed and breakfast house in the town.

"The department will take my daughter along to see the house on Monday," Mrs Wilkinson said.

And until then, Mr Herbert Jacobs, Reading housing manager, has said that she

and her four children can stay with Mrs Wilkinson until Monday.

Mrs Norma Taylor, 37, and her four children came to Reading to live near Mrs Wilkinson because she is crippled.

"So while my daughter tried to find somewhere to live nearby, I put up my four grandchildren here in the flat. I knew I was doing wrong as this was a council flat but I couldn't just turn them onto the street.

Complained

"When you're old and a widow, your grandchildren are all that is left. They were so quiet here. I bought them jig-saws to keep them occupied. Yet it seems one of my neighbours complained about the children making a noise. Now they've got to go but there's nowhere they can go," she said.

Mrs Taylor has been working in Reading for the last two weeks in the social security department's computer office. In those two weeks, she has been trying to find a flat or a house. She has

some money for a mortgage but has not yet found a house she can afford. And with four children, many flats are unavailable.

She is "almost entirely separated" from her husband. They see each other very seldom.

Mrs Wilkinson took the children into her care when their mother was ill in hospital.

"She was very ill. She almost died," she said.

When Mrs Taylor recovered she joined her children in Reading and was ready to set up home nearby when negotiations fell through.

Mr Jacobs said: "This is a bed-sitting room for one old person. We simply cannot allow five others to sleep there. Nobody would condone such overcrowding. I was astounded to hear, viz. the back door, so to speak, that this was going in.

"I have been in touch with the social services department and they are trying to find alternative accommodation for Mrs Taylor and her children.

Newspaper article 1 when homeless.

Mother plans nights in car with children

A READING mother plans to sleep in a car with her four children because she fears staying in a boarding house in the town.

Mrs Norma Taylor, 37, says that some of the people at the lodgings are violent and the language is " vile." She was placed there by Reading's social services department after fears that she was to become homeless.

But she says conditions are " terrible and sordid."

" It is costing me £36 a week for one room with one double bed, one single bed and a mattress on the floor," she said.

" It is just not the sort of place I want my children to stay at. The language is vile; somebody there threatened to commit suicide and one man almost attacked a woman."

Last week Mrs Taylor and her children were staying with her mother, Mrs Ivy Wilkinson, in a council flat without Reading housing department's knowledge.

Reading housing manager, Mr Herbert Jacobs, said they would have to leave the flat, which was designed for only one person. He arranged with the social services department for temporary accommodation for them.

Mrs Taylor came to Reading because her mother is crippled with arthritis.

She has been working for the past three weeks in the social security department's computer office. She has some money for a mortgage, but has not yet found a house she can afford. And with four children many flats are unavailable.

Rough

" I expect that as from Monday we shall be sleeping in my car. It looks very much like it.

A spokesman for Reading Social Service's Department said today: " It would be very sad if Mrs Taylor took her four children and slept in her car.

" I hope she won't do it because I would hate to think the children were going to suffer any more than they've suffered already."

She said she was doing all she could to help Mrs Taylor and was exploring "all kinds of thoughts about her case".

She denied that the boarding house was costing Mrs Taylor £36 a week.

The cost was £36, she said, but the Social Services Department paid much of that. Mrs Taylor had to pay only £12.

Newspaper article 2 when homeless.

Donna standing in the doorway to Albany Road home.

Donna at Albany Road home.

Left: Donna on her Wedding day.
Above: Mark, Donna's eldest brother who died of cancer age 56.

Chapter Seven

The Diagnosis

The shock of Hassan's diagnosis had left me reeling, incapable of comprehending the full extent of what lay ahead. Yet, as the initial wave of disbelief began to retreat, a fierce determination took hold: to arm myself with knowledge, and to confront the looming disaster of early onset Alzheimer's head-on.

With a sense of urgency driving me forward, I sought solace and understanding in the pages of every book I could lay my hands on. The local bookshop became my sanctuary, a refuge where I could immerse myself in the wealth of information that awaited within the covers of each volume. As I gathered an armful of books on the subject, I felt a surge of determination coursing through me, a resolve to leave no stone unturned in my quest for understanding.

Returning home, I embarked on a marathon of reading, devouring page after page in a desperate bid to grasp the intricacies of a disease that threatened to unravel our lives. Through the long hours of the night, I delved into the depths of each book, absorbing the grim realities that lay within. The more I learned, the more horrified I became, each revelation casting a shadow over the fragile hope that had dared to flicker within me.

The stark truth emerged with chilling clarity: early onset Alzheimer's was not just a diagnosis; it was a sentence, a cruel twist of fate that threatened to rob Hassan of not only his memories but also his very life. Unlike its later-life counterpart, this insidious disease wielded its destructive power with alarming speed, leaving little time for its victims to come to terms with their fate.

The realisation hit me like a physical blow: my beloved husband, the man I had vowed to love and cherish, might be facing a fate far worse than anything we had ever imagined. The idea of mortality loomed large, casting a shadow over our hopes and dreams, rendering them fragile in the face of such overwhelming uncertainty.

Yet, even as despair threatened to engulf me, a spark of defiance ignited within my soul. Armed with knowledge and fortified by love, I refused to surrender to despair. For even in the darkest of times, there remained a glimmer of hope—a beacon of light that refused to be extinguished, guiding us forward through the storm.

The night stretched on endlessly, a relentless cycle of anguish and exhaustion. Despite the weariness that weighed heavily upon me, sleep remained elusive, chased away by the news of Hassan's diagnosis that haunted my every thought. As the hours wore on, I found myself engulfed in a cocoon of books, their pages a refuge from the harsh realities that awaited me outside their covers.

In the dim light of the room, I poured over the words with a feverish intensity, each passage a lifeline in a sea of uncertainty. Yet, even as I sought solace in the pages before me, doubt gnawed at the edges of my consciousness. Could it truly be possible that Hassan, my beloved husband, was facing such a cruel fate?

In moments of desperation, I turned to him, seeking reassurance in the familiar contours of his face. The cognitive tests I had read about became a litmus test of sorts, a desperate bid to cling to the hope that perhaps, just perhaps, the doctor had been mistaken. Yet, with each failed attempt, the reality of our situation seemed to crystallise, a bitter pill that I struggled to swallow.

The exhaustion that gripped me, both physical and emotional, blurred the boundaries between reality and illusion. In my delirium, I found myself attempting to shoulder the burden of Hassan's decline, clumsily attempting to anticipate his needs before they even arose. His confusion mirrored my own, his voice a beacon of clarity in the fog of despair that enveloped us both.

As the night wore on, the tears flowed nonstop, a silent testament to the magnitude of our grief. The weight of unshed tears threatened to drown me, their salty taste a bitter reminder of the anguish that gnawed at my soul. In the darkness, I wrestled with my own sense of helplessness, grappling with the cruel irony of a fate that had robbed us of our dreams and aspirations.

In the quiet hours of the night, I found myself bargaining with a higher power, pleading for a reprieve from the relentless onslaught of despair. The thought of losing Hassan, of watching helplessly as the disease claimed him bit by bit, was a pain too great to bear. In my darkest moments, I found myself wishing for a different fate, for anything that would spare him the indignity of his impending deterioration.

The night stretched on, a testament to the depth of our despair, yet even amidst the darkness, a flicker of resilience remained—a stubborn refusal to surrender to the despair that threatened to consume us. For even in the bleakest of moments, love remained our anchor, a beacon of light that refused to be extinguished, guiding us forward through the storm.

The third day dawned with a relentless grip of exhaustion and anxiety, each passing moment marked by the weight of sleep deprivation that bore down upon me like a heavy cloak. Yet, despite the weariness that threatened to engulf me, a restless energy pulsed beneath the surface, propelling me forward with a frantic urgency.

In the solitude of our home, I found myself consumed by a relentless need to keep busy, to drown out the loud racket of fears and doubts that echoed within the recesses of my mind.

With trembling hands and a racing heart, I threw myself into the task of cleaning, each scrub and sweep a desperate attempt to regain a semblance of control amidst the chaos that threatened to consume me.

The hours stretched on, the rhythm of my movements a futile attempt to silence the relentless drumbeat of anxiety that echoed within me. Even as the night descended, casting shadows that danced upon the walls, I found no respite from the relentless tide of thoughts that threatened to overwhelm me.

By morning, the toll of my sleepless nights had taken its toll, manifesting in a dull ache behind my eyes and a hypersensitivity to the light that filtered through the curtains. The world outside seemed to pulsate with an intensity that bordered on overwhelming, each ray of sunlight a piercing lance that seared through my fragile defences.

Clad in sunglasses to shield my eyes from the glare, I ventured forth into the world beyond the confines of 8 Blithe Walk. The familiar sights and sounds of the street, once mundane and unremarkable, now seemed imbued with a newfound vibrancy, a kaleidoscope of sensations that attacked my senses with a dizzying intensity.

As I paused to stroke a passing dog, the warmth of its fur beneath my fingers sent a surge of warmth coursing through me, a fleeting moment of connection in a world that had felt so distant and cold. The laughter of children, the rustle of leaves in the breeze—each sight and sound served as a poignant reminder of the beauty that still existed amidst the chaos of our lives.

In that moment, as I watched the world awaken around me, I realised that I had been so consumed by grief and despair that I had forgotten to truly live. The simple joys and wonders that surrounded me, the beauty of nature and the innocence of a child's smile—these were the gifts that I had been blind to, lost amidst the turmoil of my own sorrow.

With each step forward, I felt a glimmer of hope ignite within me, a beacon of light that cut through the darkness of despair. For even in the darkest of times, there remained a flicker of possibility—a chance to rediscover the beauty and wonder that still existed within and around me. And as I walked on, bathed in the warm embrace of the sunlight, I knew that no matter how bleak the road ahead may seem, there was still beauty to be found, still hope to be cherished amidst the shadows.

As I stepped into the bustling waiting room of the doctor's surgery, the sense of connection I had experienced outside only intensified. Surrounded by a chorus of coughs and sneezes, each sound seemed to echo the pain and discomfort of those around me. With each cough, each sniffle, I felt a pang of sympathy, as if their illness had woven itself into the fabric of my being, tugging at the very core of my being.

The air was thick with the scent of antiseptic and sickness, a tangible reminder of the fragility of human health. Every movement, every sound felt magnified, heightened by the tension that hung heavy in the air. When the receptionist's pen clattered against the desk, the sudden noise jolted me, bringing my attention back from my thoughts and sending a shiver down my spine.

When at last I was ushered into the doctor's office, I struggled to articulate the overwhelming pressure behind my eyes, the sensation of being trapped beneath a suffocating weight. Yet, even as I spoke, I withheld the full extent of my symptoms, fearing that to reveal the depths of my despair would brand me as mad.

The doctor's examination yielded no tangible answers, leaving me to grapple with the gnawing uncertainty that plagued my every waking moment. With a hollow sense of resignation, I left the surgery, the weight of unspoken fears weighing heavily upon my shoulders.

As I made my way home, the world seemed to blur around me, a haze of exhaustion and anxiety clouding my vision. The journey back to 8 Blithe Walk felt impossible, each step a weary march towards an uncertain fate. Yet, even as doubt and despair threatened to consume me, a glimmer of hope remained—a stubborn refusal to surrender to the darkness that threatened to engulf me. For even in the bleakest of moments, there remained a flicker of possibility—a chance to reclaim the light that had been lost amidst the shadows.

The strange sensations that had plagued me throughout the day grew increasingly ominous, casting a pall of unease over every step I took. With each passing stranger, I found myself locked in a silent battle of wills, their eyes a window into the depths of their souls. Some emanated warmth and kindness, their essence a soothing balm to my frayed nerves. But others... Others exuded a darkness so palpable it sent a shiver down my spine.

In their gaze, I glimpsed the flicker of malevolence, a sinister presence lurking beneath the surface like a coiled serpent poised to strike. The hairs on the back of my neck prickled with apprehension, my heart pounding a frantic rhythm of fear. Hastening my pace, I averted my eyes, seeking solace in the familiar cadence of the Lord's Prayer, its comforting words a shield against the encroaching darkness.

Relief washed over me as I finally crossed the threshold of our home, seeking sanctuary from the rage within. Yet, even within the confines of familiar walls, the sense of unease lingered, a silent spectre that refused to be banished. Turning to the radio in search of distraction, I was met with static, the noise echoing the chaos that churned within my mind.

Amidst the chaos, a voice—a distorted and broken whisper—cut through the static, its message as clear as a bell. In that moment, a conviction seized hold of me, an unshakeable belief that I was being spoken to by a higher power. As the voice spoke, I felt a sense of clarity wash over me, a divine connection that transcended the boundaries of mortal understanding.

Yet, as my husband entered the room, I hastily silenced the

radio, the weight of my newfound revelation too heavy to bear in the presence of another. But even as the room fell silent, the conviction remained, a flickering flame of faith that burned bright within me. For in that fleeting moment, I had touched the divine, and nothing would ever be the same again.

As the days stretched on, my newfound connection with the divine only deepened, each passing moment a testament to the inexplicable bond that now bound me to the heavens above. The sky, once a vast expanse of blue, now seemed alive with purpose, its canvas adorned with the celestial markings of passing airplanes. In my fevered mind, each trail left behind by their passage became a beacon, a sign from above that God sought to communicate with me.

With each passing day, my senses seemed to sharpen, my gaze drawn upwards towards the heavens. The sun, once a source of discomfort, now held a magnetic allure, its radiant glow a testament to the divine presence that now took over my every thought and action.

Yet, as the nights wore on and sleep continued to elude me, the boundaries between reality and delusion blurred with alarming clarity. In the solitude of the night, I found myself consumed by a frenzied compulsion, my actions guided by a sense of purpose that defied rational explanation.

On the fifth night, my behaviour took a turn for the bizarre, my actions a testament to the depths of my fractured psyche. In the dead of night, I moved with an almost frenetic energy, my movements fuelled by a desperate need to cleanse the world around me of its perceived evils.

As my mother looked on in confusion, I found myself engaged in a strange ritual, the contents of the fridge transformed into instruments of purification. With trembling hands, I wielded a bottle of water as if it were holy, its droplets a sacrament to cleanse the tainted air of our home. With each invocation of the Lord's Prayer, I sought to banish the darkness that clung to the walls, my mind consumed by the memory of past traumas that had scarred the very fabric of our existence.

In my distorted reality, the misery and violence that had once plagued 8 Blithe Walk now manifested as an evil presence that lurked within the shadows. Driven by a firm belief in the righteousness of my cause, I embarked on a crusade to purge the darkness that threatened to consume us all. And in the solitude of the night, amidst the echoes of my own intense prayers, I found a semblance of solace—a fleeting moment of peace amidst the chaos that raged within.

As the morning light filtered through the windows, casting long shadows that seemed to dance with sinister intent, the oppressive weight of evil that hung over 8 Blithe Walk only grew more suffocating. With each passing moment, the air seemed to thicken with a palpable sense of dread, a foreboding presence that whispered of unseen horrors lurking within the walls.

Alone in the house, the silence was deafening, broken only by the faint echoes of distant memories that echoed through the empty halls. With each creak of the floorboards, my heart pounded in my chest, the sense of impending doom weighing heavy upon me like a leaden cloak.

Unable to bear the suffocating grip of fear that threatened to consume me, I fled from the confines of the house in a blind panic, my mind consumed by a primal instinct to escape. Dressed only in my pyjamas, I raced towards the main road, heedless of the dangers that lay in wait.

But just as I reached the threshold of danger, fate intervened in the form of Ray, the very embodiment of the turmoil that had plagued our lives for so long. In a twist of irony, it was he who pulled me back from the brink of disaster, his rough hands gripping me tightly as he hauled me to safety.

Yet, even as he ushered me back into the house, locking the door behind us, I felt the walls closing in around me, their suffocating embrace a stark reminder of the prison from which I longed to escape. With trembling hands, I reached for the only beacon of hope I could find: the battered gold crucifix that had once belonged to Nan, its tarnished surface a testament to the trials of a lifetime.

With the crucifix clutched tightly in my hand, I fled into the sanctuary of the garden, seeking solace amidst the chaos that raged within. With each fervent prayer that escaped my lips, I felt a semblance of peace wash over me, a fleeting moment of respite amidst the storm. For in the face of darkness, it was faith that illuminated the path forward, a beacon of hope amidst the shadows that threatened to consume us all.

As Mum returned home, her heart heavy with dread, she was met with a scene straight from the depths of her worst nightmares. Stepping into the living room, she was greeted by a sight that chilled her to the bone—a scene of utter madness unfolding before her eyes. There I was, crouched upon the floor like a wild beast, my eyes ablaze with a primal fury that seemed to defy all reason. To her horror, it appeared as though I had become possessed by some evil force, my very essence consumed by darkness.

With a gasp of disbelief, my mother recoiled in shock, her mind struggling to comprehend the horrors that lay before her. "Oh my god, Donna," she exclaimed, her voice trembling with fear and desperation. "We need to get you help, now."

As we embarked on the journey to the GP, the world around me seemed to warp and distort, taking on the nightmarish quality of a horror film. Everywhere I turned, I was confronted by visions of evil, the darkness lurking within the eyes of passers-by casting a sinister glow over the world. A child on a bicycle, his face twisted into an eerie expression, seemed to defy the laws of reality as he pedalled backwards, dragging with him a surreal procession of figures moving in reverse.

Overwhelmed by the grotesque spectacle unfolding around me, I squeezed my eyes shut, desperate to block out the twisted visions that threatened to consume my sanity. In the depths of my despair, I grasped for the lifeline of faith that had sustained me in times of trouble before. With each whispered repetition of the words "Love, light, and peace," I sought to rekindle the connection with the divine that had once filled me with hope and solace. For in the darkness that threatened to engulf me, it was the light of faith that offered the faintest glimmer of salvation.

As we embarked on the journey to Prospect Park Psychiatric Hospital, the world outside seemed to warp and contort, its familiar contours twisted into grotesque shapes by the grip of my delusions. With each passing moment, the road ahead seemed to stretch endlessly before us, the other vehicles crowding in around us like wicked phantoms, intent on ruining our divine mission.

In the corners of my mind, I felt a sense of certainty wash over me; a conviction that our destination held the promise of salvation, a gateway to the heavenly realm beyond. With each passing mile, I felt the hand of God guiding us forward, his divine presence a beacon of hope amidst the darkness that threatened to consume us.

Arriving at Prospect Park Psychiatric Hospital, I was filled with a sense of euphoria, the anticipation of meeting my maker pulsing through my veins like a fevered dream. As we waited in the reception area, I felt a surge of elation wash over me, my heart soaring with the knowledge that I was on the cusp of a divine revelation.

When at last we were ushered into a room, I was met by the figure of a woman—a psychiatrist, dressed in a smart navy suit with blonde hair bouncing around her shoulders. In that moment, I felt an overwhelming rush of emotion flood through me, a profound sense of gratitude and love that seemed to transcend earthly bounds.

"Are you God?" I asked her, my voice trembling with awe. But her response was merely a gentle smile, her eyes betraying no hint of the divine presence I had expected to find.

Undeterred by her silence, I rose from my seat, my heart brimming with an unshakeable faith. "I am Jesus," I proclaimed, my words heavy with a sense of purpose that burned like a fire within me. "I am here to save the world."

In that moment, as I stood before the psychiatrist, I felt the weight of my divine calling pressing down upon me—a sacred duty to bring light to the darkness, to cast out the demons that plagued the world and usher in a new era of peace and salvation. And though the world around me remained unchanged, I knew that within the depths of my soul, a divine purpose awaited, beckoning me forward on a path illuminated by the light of faith.

As the doctor led me through the motions of the examination, each mundane task took on a weighty significance in my fevered mind. When she mentioned weighing me, I felt a shiver of dread course through my veins, convinced that the scales held the key to my fate, my worthiness to ascend to the heavens or be cast down into the abyss.

In a frenzy of panic, I stripped away my clothes, desperate to shed any excess weight that might tip the scales against me. In that moment, every ounce of my being was consumed by the fear of judgment, the spectre of divine scrutiny looming large over my trembling form.

But as the doctor gently coaxed me back into my clothes, her soothing words offering a semblance of reassurance, I clung to the fragile hope that I had passed some unseen trial, earning my place among the celestial hosts.

As we made our way to the ward, however, the illusion began to unravel, giving way to a new wave of terror. In the depths of my delusion, I sensed a malevolent presence lurking in the shadows, its tendrils of darkness reaching out to ensnare me in its grasp.

Clinging to my mother's side, I pleaded for her protection, my mind consumed by visions of impending doom. Even the most mundane tasks, like using the restroom, became fraught with peril, each moment fraught with the fear of being dragged down into the depths of hell.

In that moment of vulnerability, my mind teetered on the brink of madness, its fragile grasp on reality slipping away like grains of sand through an open hand. And as I stood on the precipice, staring into the abyss, I prayed for salvation, desperately clinging to the flickering light of hope in the face of overwhelming darkness.

As I stood before the sink, the harsh light of the hospital bathroom casting distorted shadows across my face, I found myself transfixed by the reflection staring back at me. In the depths of my own eyes, I glimpsed a darkness—a malevolent force lurking just beneath the surface, waiting to consume me whole.

In that moment, it felt as though the demon that had haunted me in the living room had returned, its grip tightening around my soul with each passing second. The urge to purge myself of its influence consumed me, a desperate desire to rid myself of the darkness that threatened to engulf me entirely.

But try as I might, I found myself paralysed, unable to escape the suffocating embrace of the demon within. With each laboured breath, its presence loomed larger, casting a shadow over my fragile sanity.

"Come on, love," my mother's voice cut through the haze of my terror, pulling me back from the brink. "We've got to go to the ward now."

With a sense of dread gnawing at my insides, I followed her down the corridor, my movements disjointed and animalistic, like a creature possessed. As we approached the waiting doctor, I felt the weight of impending doom pressing down upon me, the door to the ward looming ominously in the distance like a gateway to the abyss.

"Mum, please, don't leave me," I pleaded, my grip on her sleeve tightening with desperation as she guided me through the doorway. Despite my trembling limbs and racing heart, she pressed forward, her reassuring presence the only anchor in the swirling chaos of my mind.

As we entered the room, a new wave of terror washed over me, the walls closing in around me like the jaws of some unseen predator. In a crazy outburst, the words spilled from my lips like venom, a twisted confession torn from the depths of my fractured psyche.

"I've been raped by the devil!" I cried out, my voice echoing off the sterile walls of the room, each syllable laced with raw anguish and despair. But my words fell on deaf ears, drowned out by the sounds of my own torment.

Before I knew it, I was surrounded by a flurry of activity, the faces of the hospital staff blurring together in a whirlwind of motion. Needles pierced my skin, drugs coursed through my veins, and the world faded into darkness as unconsciousness claimed me at last.

In that moment of blessed oblivion, I welcomed the respite from the torment that had consumed me, if only for a fleeting moment. And as the darkness enveloped me, I surrendered to its embrace, grateful to escape the clutches of my own fractured mind, if only for a while.

In the haze of medication and delusion, my days blurred together into an indistinct tapestry of light and shadow, joy and despair. Sedated and adrift in a sea of confusion, I floated between two opposing realms of existence, each vying for dominance within the corners of my fractured mind.

Within the confines of my small, sterile room, devoid of adornment save for the NHS blue curtains and gleaming linoleum floor, I grappled with the thought of suicide that loomed over me like a shadow, a constant reminder of the fragility of my fractured psyche.

Yet amid the chaos, there were moments of fleeting clarity, shards of lucidity that pierced through the fog of my delusions. I soon realised that I was under constant surveillance, confined to my room as I teetered on the edges of self-destruction.

In my manic highs, I became convinced of my divine purpose, convinced that I had been chosen to bear a child destined to save humanity. My longing for motherhood morphed into a delusional belief that I carried the offspring of God within me, a messianic figure destined to usher in a new era of salvation.

At other times, I found myself consumed by the belief that I was the Messiah incarnate, my hands bearing the phantom wounds of stigmata, a testament to my divine nature. Desperate for validation, I turned to my friends for reassurance, seeking solace in their presence amidst the turmoil in my mind.

But their hesitant glances and awkward exchanges only served to deepen my isolation, their well-meaning attempts to dismiss my delusions falling on deaf ears. As I grappled with the chasm between reality and fantasy, I clung to the fragile threads of sanity, praying for deliverance from the darkness that threatened to consume me whole.

After undergoing an MRI at the Royal Berkshire Hospital, the doctors confirmed that there were no physical abnormalities in my brain that could explain my severe psychosis. This revelation led me back to the familiar confines of Bluebell Wing, where I began to tentatively explore the new world around me.

My room, while not locked, still felt like a cell, a sterile sanctuary within the labyrinthine corridors of the psychiatric ward. Venturing out into the communal areas, I encountered my fellow patients, each grappling with their own demons as they sought solace within the confines of our shared reality.

In the common room, the flickering glow of the television cast a pale light over the faces of those gathered, their eyes fixed on the screen in silent daydream. The kitchen, a hive of activity, buzzed with the chatter of patients as they brewed cups of tea and coffee, seeking comfort in the warmth of shared companionship.

As I ventured further, I stumbled upon the Activity Room, its door a portal to a world of shared experiences and collective healing. Through the glass window, I watched as patients sat in a circle, their voices mingling in a symphony of shared stories and shared struggles.

Amidst this whirlwind of activity, a middle-aged woman approached me, her eyes filled with a mixture of confusion and concern.

"Oh hello," she said. "You really frightened me when you came in. You kissed me on the cheek and told me you loved me!"

Her words washed over me, and I struggled to recall the encounter she described. Had I really kissed her on the cheek and professed my love? The memory eluded me, slipping through my fingers like grains of sand. I couldn't recall the encounter she described, and the details of my presence in the hospital remained elusive. But then, like a sudden revelation, the memories flooded back, filling the void with a newfound clarity.

Yes, I was here for a reason; a purpose ordained by a higher power. God had chosen me, a vessel for divine intervention, tasked with saving the world from an impending catastrophe. The hospital, once a symbol of confinement, now served as a sanctuary—a place where I could fulfil my sacred duty to protect the caretakers of humanity.

In my mind's eye, I saw war, a global conflict poised to engulf the world in chaos and despair. But amidst the darkness, a glimmer of hope emerged—a beacon of salvation in the form of the doctors and nurses who tirelessly struggled to preserve life in the face of adversity.

With renewed determination, I embraced my role as a harbinger of peace, resolved to rally the forces of good against the encroaching tide of destruction. For in the crucible of my delusions, I found purpose—a guiding light to navigate the tumultuous waters of my fractured mind. And though the path ahead was filled with uncertainty, I marched forward with unwavering faith, ready to confront whatever challenges lay in wait.

My gaze swept across the room, and I noticed a nurse, her steps brisk and purposeful, slipping into a sanctuary labelled "Staff Room". A pulse of urgency propelled me forward, and I darted after her, my hand catching the door just as it whispered a breath away from closure.

"You can't come in here, it's staff only," she declared, her voice a firm barrier to my mission.

"I am staff!" I retorted with a desperation that surprised even me. Didn't they understand? I was on a divine assignment, an emissary of a higher calling. How could I allow mere protocols to defeat my purpose? I was not merely a cog in the machine; I was working for God, tasked with a mission of utmost importance.

With a passion born of my conviction, I attempted to shoulder past her, my words escalating into a plea, a demand to be allowed passage.

"You must let me through!" I insisted, my voice edging into desperation. Yet, my plea seemed to summon a force against me. The commotion, a situation of my own making, rippled through the corridors, drawing others to the fray.

Before I fully grasped the shift in the tide, I was engulfed by a sea of uniforms, bodies of staff members who materialised as if summoned by an unseen alarm. They converged on me with a practiced efficiency, their hands firm and unyielding. I twisted and turned, a wild tempest of limbs, fuelled by a blend of panic and an unshakeable belief in my cause.

Then, amidst the chaos, a sharp pinch in my thigh; the cold kiss of a needle. As the liquid fire spread through my veins, the world began to dim, and my struggles faded away. The last thing I felt was the embrace of oblivion, swallowing me whole, as everything went to black.

In the ensuing days, a semblance of tranquillity began to weave itself into the fabric of my being, though the tendrils of my delusions still lingered, whispering their deceitful tales from the shadowy corners of my mind. Amidst this inner turmoil, I discovered a sanctuary within the hospital's walls: the chapel. It became my refuge, a place where I could lay bare my soul and seek solace in prayer. The intensity of my petitions grew with each visit, especially when the murky sensation of malevolence threatened to envelop me once more.

My reliance on this sacred space was never more evident than on a day when the ordinary clatter of the kitchen morphed into a harbinger of darkness. The simple act of pans tumbling from a shelf set my heart racing, their metallic crash echoing like sinister laughter through the corridors of my mind. Convinced that this was no accident but the manoeuvrings of an evil spirit, I was seized by an uncontrollable urge to flee. Panic took hold, propelling me through the hospital with a single-minded focus: to reach the sanctuary of the chapel.

As I dashed through the wards, my shouts of a haunted ward bounced off the walls, a frantic warning that left a trail of confusion and alarm in my wake. My announcement that an unseen, malevolent presence lurked among us stirred a wave of unrest among the patients. Many, already ensnared by their own battles with unseen enemies, were thrust deeper into the grip of their fears by my panicked cries.

The ripple effect of my outburst was palpable, casting a shadow over the hospital as staff and patients alike grappled with the heightened tension. In the aftermath, as calm was painstakingly restored, I found myself once more in the quietude of the chapel, wrestling with the guilt of having disturbed the fragile peace of my fellow sufferers. Yet, in the silence of that holy place, I continued to seek the strength to face the phantoms of my mind, hoping for the day when the whispers of delusion would finally be silenced.

Among the abundance of souls that populated the hospital, Derek emerged as a figure both endearing and enigmatic. A frail, elderly gentleman cloaked perpetually in an anorak, despite the controlled temperature within the hospital walls. His presence was a constant, a quiet force that seemed untouched by the chaos that sometimes unfolded around us.

Our paths converged over the shared ritual of lunch, amid my fervent musings that one of the doctors might secretly embody the divine. It was then I posed a question that had been circling my thoughts like a persistent moth: what did God look like? Derek, with the gentle patience of someone who had weathered many storms, admitted he did not know. Yet, he held firm to one belief: the sanctity of keeping the Bible elevated, a principle he demonstrated with a small, well-thumbed book he treasured above all else. This act, simple in its execution but profound in its intention, resonated deeply with me. In Derek, I saw not just a friend but a kindred spirit, someone whose convictions mirrored my own search for meaning in a world that often felt beyond comprehension.

Our bond was immediate and unwavering. Derek, with his forgetful, distant gaze that mirrored the one I had seen in another's eyes, might have been navigating the fog of Alzheimer's. This shared vulnerability drew me even closer to him, forging between us a connection that transcended the spoken word. I became his anchor, a point of certainty in the shifting sands of his reality. Wherever I went, Derek was my shadow, a silent affirmation that even in our isolation, we had found a semblance of belonging.

The world beyond the hospital's confines seemed to have forgotten Derek, leaving no trace of family or friends to visit him. This abandonment only tightened the bond between us, for in my relatives' absence, Derek found solace in the edges of my world, often seen wandering the corridors with a forlorn air or peering through the window of the visitors' room, seeking the warmth of a connection he no longer had. In those moments, our friendship became not just a comfort, but a lifeline, affirming that even in the most unlikely places, companionship and understanding can flourish.

In the intricate dance of our daily lives within the hospital, I had inadvertently stepped into a role that felt both familiar and essential: caring for Derek as I had once envisioned caring for my husband. This unexpected turn of events lent my own turmoil a semblance of purpose, weaving a thread of meaning through the fabric of my illness. The chaos that had unravelled my sense of self was intimately tied to Hassan's diagnosis, a storm that had swept me into a realm where I clung to the belief that I was not the one in need of care. In this conviction, I found solace in tending to Derek, a tangible way to anchor myself against the pull of my own disarray.

Our routine became a small island of normalcy in the swirling sea of the hospital's madness. I took it upon myself to cut Derek's food, to prepare for him a peculiar concoction that was his favourite—a blend of tea and coffee. Within the walls of our temporary home, this odd mixture became a symbol of our shared defiance against convention, a small act of rebellion that made sense only to us. It wasn't long before I, too, found comfort in this unique brew, a testament to the ways in which Derek had influenced my life in return.

The news of my impending transfer to another ward struck with the force of an unexpected blow, severing the connection I had found with Derek. The doctors' explanation did little to ease the pain of separation; a mere administrative oversight had placed me in Bluebell Ward instead of Daisy, where I rightfully belonged. The realisation that I would be torn away from the person who had become my ward mate, my friend, and the focus of my nurturing instincts left me reeling. Our shared moments, the comfort we found in each other's company, suddenly seemed fragile against the impersonal decisions of hospital administration.

In that moment, the prospect of leaving Derek behind was more than just a change of scenery—it was a profound loss, a disconnection from the one person who had become a beacon of light in the disorienting darkness of my illness. The thought of navigating the days ahead without him, without our routines and the silent understanding that had grown between us, filled me with a sense of desolation. As I faced the reality of our separation, the hospital, with its endless corridors and sterile rooms, seemed all the more daunting, a labyrinth from which the path to healing had become uncertain.

The transition to the new ward was like stepping into a tempest, a stark departure from the relative calm of Bluebell. The air was thick with tension, punctuated by the cacophony of shouting and the undercurrent of illicit dealings that permeated the space. Gone was the tranquil sanctuary I had found in Bluebell, replaced instead with a place where peace seemed a foreign concept. Most acutely felt was the absence of Derek, whose quiet companionship had been a steadying presence in my life. His absence left a void that the chaos around me seemed eager to fill.

Compelled by a sense of desperation, I sought out the doctor, my resolve as clear as the words I spoke. I asserted my status as a voluntary patient, clinging to the sliver of autonomy it afforded me. My declaration that I would not remain in this tumultuous environment was fuelled by a newfound clarity. Though the edges of my reality were still blurred, the delusions that had once clouded my judgement had receded, leaving me on a precipice between my past confusion and the uncertain promise of normalcy.

The doctors, perhaps sensing my resolve, underscored the importance of continuing my medication regimen before my departure. They laid bare the diagnosis that had been a shadow companion through my journey: a hypomanic episode with acute polymorphic psychosis. Their words painted a picture of a path that could easily spiral into a cycle of return if I wasn't vigilant. The term "revolving-door patient" echoed in my mind, a future I was determined to avoid.

Hassan's arrival was a beacon of hope, a tangible link to the world beyond the hospital's confines. As the nurses transported my belongings to the car, each item served as a marker of the time spent within these walls. The pots from the activity room, the personal effects my mother had brought to brighten my days—all were physical remnants of a chapter that was closing. Prospect Park Psychiatric Hospital, with its contradictions and challenges, had become a peculiar home, a place of healing and turmoil intertwined.

Departing without a farewell to Derek was a regret that hung heavily on my heart. His story, like mine, had become an integral part of the hospital, but the threads of our narratives were diverging. The possibility of his release, or the lack thereof, remained an unanswered question—a lingering connection to a place that had shaped us both. As we drove away, the hospital receded into the background, a chapter concluded but not forgotten, its lessons and legacies imprinted on the journey ahead.

The spectre of my delusions had been banished, a victory owed to the meticulous regimen of medication that had become the cornerstone of my existence. The home care team, a group of diligent guardians, frequented my doorstep, ensuring I remained tethered to this newfound stability. Yet, beneath the surface of this apparent calm, my psyche remained a fragile construct, teetering on the brink of disarray.

The environment at home, far from being a sanctuary, had transformed into an arena of tension. The presence of Ray and Kevin, once perhaps negligible or merely inconvenient, now loomed large and oppressive. Their existence in my space, a space I so desperately needed to be safe and nurturing, became a source of constant agitation. The irony was palpable; I had emerged from the confines of a mental institution only to find the atmosphere at home equally suffocating. No corner of my world offered solace or respite; I was adrift, longing for a haven that seemed ever elusive.

The breaking point came, not with a whisper but with a decisive action by Mum. Witnessing the detrimental effect Ray and Kevin had on my fragile state, she took a stand. Her directive for them to leave was a declaration of her priorities, a clear assertion that my well-being was paramount.

"Why should we go?" Ray shouted, drunkenly.

"Because," Mum replied, "Donna's been really unwell, and she can't cope with this anymore."

"Well then she's the one who should go," Ray had said. "Lock her up!"

His words, a drunken slur, sought to invert the logic of the situation, suggesting that I, the one in recovery, should be the one to leave, to be "locked up" once more.

This exchange, though painful, was revelatory. It shed light on the stark contrast between those who truly understood the nature of my struggle and those who, either through ignorance or indifference, refused to acknowledge the gravity of my condition. The suggestion to exile me, to send me back to an institution, was a chilling reminder of the stigma and misunderstanding that still surrounds mental health. In that moment, the battle lines were drawn not just within the confines of our home, but within the broader context of my journey towards healing—a journey fraught with challenges but also illuminated by the possibility of finding a true sense of belonging and peace.

Mum's unwavering stance eventually wore them, leading to the departure of Ray and Kevin. Their exit, though a relief, did not signify the beginning of a peaceful chapter as one might have hoped. Instead, it left a void that was quickly filled by an approaching shadow of depression. The absence of their turmoil did little to alleviate the weight of my own internal battles. As I languished in the confines of my bed, the echoes of the past mingled with the dread of an uncertain future, drawing me deeper into despair.

The possibility of becoming a revolving-door patient, a term that had once seemed like a distant warning, now loomed over me with a sense of inevitability. Each day blended into the next, a monotonous cycle of reflection and sorrow, punctuated by the gradual decline of Hassan's health. The progression of his Alzheimer's served as a grim reminder of the relentless march of time and the diseases that follow in its wake. The future, once a horizon teeming with possibilities, now appeared barren and devoid of hope.

In a moment of sheer desperation, overwhelmed by the bleakness of our situation, I found myself voicing a thought that had taken root in the darkest corners of my mind.

"Hassan," I begged him. "Let's just end it now. We can gas ourselves in the car."

The suggestion to end our suffering, to seek an escape from the pain and uncertainty that had engulfed us, was born from a place of profound despair. Yet, Hassan's response, a silent but firm refusal, was a testament to a will to endure that I had struggled to find within myself.

His decision to share my dark proposition with the care worker during their next visit was a pivotal moment. It was an act of intervention, a plea for help on my behalf that I couldn't voice myself. This moment of transparency, though it felt like a betrayal at the time, was perhaps the lifeline I needed. It opened the door to conversations about the depth of my despair, a crucial step towards seeking the support and intervention necessary to navigate the treacherous waters of mental illness. In revealing my thoughts, Hassan inadvertently set us on a path towards healing, towards finding a sliver of light in the overwhelming darkness that had threatened to consume us.

It was in this moment that I realised I would have to find a way to end my suffering without Hassan. Thus, in the solitude of our home, with the world unaware and distant, I found myself at a crossroads of despair.

The note I penned to Hassan was both a farewell and an apology, a final attempt to articulate a pain that had grown too immense to bear. The details of my bank account, a mundane inclusion amidst the enormity of my decision, were meant to ensure that he would have one less burden to navigate in my absence. With each word, I hoped to convey a love that remained untarnished by the darkness that had enveloped my mind.

The concoction of psychiatric medication, each pill a testament to my battles, seemed to offer a silent promise of release. As I settled into the bath, the warmth of the water enveloping me, a surreal calm took hold. The act, far removed from a plea for salvation, was a resigned acceptance of defeat—an overwhelming desire to escape a world that had become unbearable.

Lingering in the threshold between consciousness and oblivion, a curious thought flickered through my fading awareness. The logistics of a soul's departure, bound by the physical constraints of a shut window, sparked a fleeting wonder. Would my spirit remain ensnared within the confines of 8 Blithe Walk, a silent witness to the life I was leaving behind? The notion of being trapped, even in death, mirrored the entrapment I felt in life, a poignant reflection of my struggle to find peace.

This moment of introspection, however brief, underscored the complexity of the human spirit's yearning for release. The decision to end one's life, made in the depths of despair, carried with it questions that remained unanswered, fears that persisted beyond the final breath. It's a reminder of the invisible chains that bound us, not just to our physical existence, but to the places and memories that define us. In the end, the quest for peace—a peace that seemed so elusive in life—remained intertwined with the very essence of my being, a testament to the enduring hope that, perhaps, beyond the pain and turmoil, a semblance of tranquillity awaited.

The unexpected interruption of the doorbell, a sound I had completely overlooked in my state of despair, became the inadvertent saviour that pulled me back from the precipice. The home treatment team, whose visit I had not anticipated, became the unforeseen force that intervened in my darkest moment. If the home treatment team discovered the note I had hastily left on the side table, they would immediately understand the depth of my despair and likely decide to readmit me to Prospect Park Psychiatric Hospital for further care.

With every ounce of willpower I could muster, I dragged myself out from the water's embrace, destroying the tangible evidence of my intent before succumbing to the overwhelming lethargy that had begun to claim me.

Awakening in an unfamiliar environment, with the concerned face of a stranger hovering into view, my disoriented mind grappled with the reality of my situation. The question that escaped my lips, "Am I in heaven?" was a reflection of my longing for peace, for an end to the relentless turmoil that had characterised my existence.

His reply, though gentle, anchored me back to a reality I had sought to escape: "No, you're in the Royal Berkshire Hospital."

The realisation that my attempt had not led to the release I had sought but had instead returned me to the realm of the living was a bitter pill to swallow. The disappointment that welled up within me was not just for the failure of my plan but for the return to a life that seemed devoid of solace or understanding.

Yet, this moment of awakening in the hospital also represented a crossroads, an opportunity to confront the pain and despair with a new perspective. It was a chance to recognise the presence of individuals who were invested in my wellbeing, even when I had felt most alone. The care worker's timely arrival, the medical staff's efforts to stabilise me—all were testaments to a network of support that existed, even in moments when it felt like all was lost.

At this particular juncture in my life, as painful and jarring as the experiences were, they served as a catalyst for initiating crucial conversations about mental health, shedding light on the profound importance of reaching out for help and addressing the underlying causes of despair. This period highlighted the intricate and complex nature of the journey towards mental healing—a path often marked by numerous setbacks, yet also highlighted by significant moments of intervention, understanding, and compassionate care.

This pivotal event in my life brought to the forefront the reality that mental well-being is not a destination, but a continuous process that demands patience, resilience, and the courage to confront one's deepest fears and vulnerabilities. It emphasised the necessity of dismantling the stigma surrounding mental health issues, encouraging an environment where seeking help is not seen as a sign of weakness but as a step towards recovery and self-discovery.

The aftermath of this challenging time was filled with uncertainty and daunting challenges, yet it was also imbued with the potential for profound personal transformation and a renewed hope for the future. It opened up avenues for deeper introspection and a better understanding of the intrinsic value of life, highlighting the possibilities for positive change and growth. This phase taught me the importance of nurturing one's mental health, of being kind and patient with oneself, and of the power of supportive relationships and open communication in facilitating healing and fostering a stronger, more resilient self.

In navigating the complexities of this journey, I learned that healing was not linear, and that setbacks were part of the process rather than indicators of failure. Each step forward, no matter how small, represented progress and a commitment to a healthier, more hopeful future. It was a journey of rediscovering joy, of opening up to love and possibility, and of stepping boldly into a future where mental well-being is prioritised and cherished.

Chapter Eight

The Great Depression

As time unfolded, it seemed to stretch endlessly, each day blending into the next in a monotonous and unyielding procession. While the acute crisis of ending my life had settled, what replaced it was a constant sense of hopelessness and depression that seemed to anchor me to my bed. This retreat to a world of isolation, a pattern reminiscent of my teenage years, became my refuge and my prison, a way to evade the outside world yet also a reminder of the depths of my despair.

Amid this struggle, there was a glimmer of understanding and support from an unexpected source. Chris, my manager, emerged as a beacon of kindness in a sea of turmoil. His visits, marked by genuine concern and an offer of unwavering support, were a lifeline during my darkest hours. The Prudential, the place of my employment, had shown a remarkable level of compassion, keeping my position open and affirming their willingness to welcome me back when I was ready. This gesture, though heartening, also became a source of internal conflict.

The thought of returning to work, to stepping back into a world that had continued in my absence, was daunting. The stigma of having been a patient in a mental health facility loomed large, casting a shadow over the prospect of reintegrating into my professional life. The fear of judgment, of whispers and sideways glances, weighed heavily on me. It wasn't just about returning to a job; it was about facing a reality in which my struggles were no longer private, where my most vulnerable moments might define me in the eyes of others.

This internal battle, between the desire to move forward and the fear of facing the perceived judgment of my colleagues, encapsulated the broader challenge of recovering from a mental health crisis. It emphasised on the complexity of healing, where physical presence in the world again required not just overcoming internal barriers but also confronting societal stigmas and misconceptions about mental health.

Continuing to dwell on Hassan's diagnosis and the turmoil enveloping my life while isolated at home served no beneficial purpose. I recognised the necessity of re-establishing a routine and reintegrating into a semblance of normalcy through my employment. Drawing inspiration from my mother, who had historically leaned into her work commitments as a coping mechanism through our family's upheavals, I decided to emulate her resilience. Therefore, after a hiatus of eight months, I mustered the courage to return to my professional life.

The experience of stepping back into the office environment proved to be intensely challenging. It seemed as though my colleagues, perhaps out of embarrassment or uncertainty on how to approach me, kept their distance, making no effort to engage in conversation. Fortunately, the presence of Kay, a dear and steadfast friend, provided a much-needed source of comfort and encouragement during this trying time.

Kay's counsel was straightforward yet empowering: "Just ignore it, Donna," she suggested, urging me to proceed as though the awkwardness around me was non-existent. "You're doing so well," she affirmed, offering a reminder of the strength I had demonstrated by simply showing up. Her support was a beacon, guiding me through the initial discomfort of reintegration and reinforcing the idea that perseverance, even in the face of adversity, was key to overcoming the challenges ahead.

Despite Kay's reassurances, I couldn't fully embrace the sentiment behind her words. The ordeal of battling psychosis had left my mind in a state of profound fragility, casting shadows of doubt over my abilities and self-assurance. It felt as though I was at the threshold of my career once again, grappling with shattered confidence and a disconnection from the knowledge and skills I once took for granted. The path ahead seemed daunting, not merely a continuation of my professional journey, but a complete rebuilding from the ground up.

In this landscape of uncertainty, Chris emerged as a beacon of understanding and patience. Recognising the depth of my struggle, he arranged for me to be retrained in my previous role, a gesture that underscored the supportive environment I found myself in. Through this process of relearning and reacquainting myself with tasks that had once been second nature, the pieces of my professional identity began to slowly find their places once again.

The journey back to a semblance of normalcy was punctuated with reminders of the person I had been prior to my illness. The realisation dawned on me that the essence of who I was might have irrevocably changed. The experiences that had tested my limits also reshaped my perspective, altering how I viewed myself and the world around me. Although I might never fully reclaim the sense of self I possessed before my battle with mental illness, the progress I made in reengaging with the everyday functions of life offered a form of solace. It was a testament to my resilience, an acknowledgment that, despite the changes within me, I was finding a way to navigate and function within the normal world once more.

Navigating the path to recovery in the workplace was just one facet of the challenges I faced; my personal life presented its own tumultuous landscape. The brief respite we had achieved by securing separate living arrangements for Ray and Kevin was now under threat. The local Council, upon discovering that Kevin had taken up residence in Ray's one-bedroom flat, was on the verge of evicting him. This predicament left us grappling with two dire options: reintroduce Kevin into our home, potentially destabilising the fragile equilibrium of my mental health, or face the guilt and worry of knowing he might end up homeless during the harsh winter months.

Complicating this situation further was the history that marred my brother's relationship with the Council housing. Previous accommodations provided to him had become hubs of illicit activity, culminating in a police raid that saw his heroin-dealer acquaintances and him expelled from the property. The aftermath of such chaos left a blemish on his record, making the plea for additional housing support from the authorities a difficult, if not impossible, endeavour.

This confluence of family dynamics and external pressures served as a constant pull away from the strides I was making in other areas of my life. The delicate balance I strove to maintain was perpetually at risk, overshadowed by the looming crisis of Kevin's living situation. Each day brought with it the heavy burden of navigating these troubled waters, searching for a solution that would safeguard my recovery without casting my brother into the cold.

Amidst the complexities of my own recovery, the plight of my brother carved out a space of profound concern within me. Understanding that his entanglement with substance abuse did not strip him of his humanity or his rights, I took upon myself the mantle of his advocate. His challenges with literacy meant that navigating the bureaucratic labyrinth of housing applications and appeals was a task he couldn't undertake alone. Thus, my commitment to his cause became an extension of my daily life.

Evenings that might have been spent in rest and recuperation were now dedicated to drafting letters to the Council, each word a plea for understanding and compassion. My lunch breaks transformed into opportunities for advocacy as I stepped away from the office to engage in phone calls with officials, each conversation a delicate dance of persuasion and persistence. The intensity of these efforts culminated in attending meetings, armed with a folder brimming with documents that chronicled my brother's situation. I stood before panels, imploring them to see beyond the surface, to recognise the individual in need beneath the stigma of addiction.

This endeavour, while a testament to familial loyalty, unfolded against the backdrop of my recent return to work following a significant mental health crisis. The dual pressures of professional responsibilities and the vigorous campaign for my brother's rights began to exact a heavy toll. The stress, a relentless undercurrent, threatened to undermine the strides I had made in my own healing journey. Navigating these concurrent challenges, I was acutely aware of the fine line I walked, striving to secure a better future for my brother while guarding the fragile peace I had fought so hard to achieve within myself.

As if the challenges I was already facing weren't enough, the festive season brought with it a new wave of family turmoil. Ray, whose health had been in decline due to cirrhosis of the liver, exacerbated by a long history of drinking, faced a dire turn in his condition. His expulsion from the family home had seemingly accelerated his descent, with his drinking habits becoming more destructive and his health rapidly deteriorating. The physical manifestations of his illness, from the blackening of his feet due to advanced diabetes to the complete failure of his liver, painted a grim picture of his situation. The inevitable hospitalisation loomed over us, a stark reminder of the consequences of a life consumed by addiction.

The burden of guilt weighed heavily on me, as I couldn't shake the feeling that my actions had contributed to Ray's worsening state. In an attempt to provide some comfort, I found myself shopping for new pyjamas and slippers, small tokens to offer him a semblance of care and normalcy as he faced the sterile environment of the hospital. However, before I could deliver these items, an urgent call in the night from Kevin disrupted any plans we had made. Ray's condition had declined so precipitously that he required immediate medical intervention, leading to his rushed admission to the hospital. The toxins that his failing liver could no longer filter were now affecting his brain, plunging him into a world of hallucinations and confusion.

This development was a harrowing reminder of the fragility of life and the devastating impact of addiction, not just on the individual but on the entire family. As I processed the news, the complexity of my emotions—guilt, sorrow, and a desperate wish for his recovery—underscored the profound challenges we faced as a family. Ray's health crisis served as a poignant reflection of the broader struggles we endured, marking yet another chapter in the ongoing saga of our family's attempts to navigate the tumultuous waters of illness, addiction, and the bonds that hold us together despite it all.

The urgency of the situation propelled Mum and me through the hospital's labyrinthine corridors until we found ourselves at the threshold of the ward where Ray lay. The ominous sound of his laboured breathing served as a grim beacon, guiding us to his bedside. The scene that greeted us was one of stark desolation: Ray, ensnared in the merciless grip of his illness, was a shadow of the man he once was. The yellow tint of his skin and its paper-like fragility painted a harrowing picture of his condition.

Kevin, whose relationship with Ray had been marred by strife and discord, was now a portrait of raw anguish. The sight of Ray, so diminished and vulnerable, struck a chord of deep sorrow within him, a testament to the complex web of emotions that familial bonds can evoke, even in the most troubled of relationships.

Ray's faint acknowledgment of my presence, his attempt at normalcy with his rasping "Alright, babe?" was a heart-wrenching reminder of the person who still lingered beneath the veneer of his illness.

"Yes. Are you alright, Ray?" I replied.

"Yeah," he rasped, still struggling to breathe.

"Oh Ray, I still care about you," cried Mum, clutching at his hand. "I can't bear to see you like this."

Kevin began crying like a baby. "Why can't they give him a liver transplant? It isn't fair," he wailed.

Facing my brother's grief and despair, I found myself at a loss for words. The harsh reality was that Ray's years of alcohol abuse had left him ineligible for a liver transplant—a lifeline denied to him due to the very choices that had led to this dire juncture. The medical team had been unequivocal in their prognosis, sparing no illusions about the limited time Ray had left. This truth, as stark and unforgiving as it was, underscored the devastating consequences of addiction, not just on the individual but on the entire fabric of a family.

"Oh Ray, I'm sorry for everything," said Kevin.

Wiping the tears away, he took some cash out of his pocket and slipped it into Ray's pyjama pocket. "Here's that £14 I owe you," he said.

In a poignant, if somewhat clumsy, effort to offer solace, Kevin reached for a small Bible tucked away in the bedside drawer. His voice, uncertain but earnest, broke the heavy silence of the hospital room as he attempted to read passages aloud to Ray. It was a gesture laden with desperation, a brother's heartfelt attempt to provide comfort, or perhaps seek redemption, in the face of impending loss.

Ray's response, though, was quintessentially him: blunt and devoid of sentimentality. With a laborious turn of his head and a voice rasped from the depths of his failing body, he dismissed

Kevin's efforts with a terse directive to "fuck off." In the starkness of that hospital room, amidst the gravity of the moment, Ray's reaction was a jarring yet fitting testament to the man he had been, unfiltered and uncompromising to the end.

Those words, stark and unadorned, marked what would be our final exchange with Ray. As the hours waned, so too did his strength, until the fight within him could no longer stave off the inevitable. By the next day, Ray had slipped away, leaving behind a silence that spoke volumes of the complex, often troubled, but undeniably human life he had led.

In the aftermath of Ray's passing, the depth of emotion that surged through the hospital room was palpable. Mum's reaction, a visceral outpouring of grief, was a stark reminder of the complex nature of human relationships. Despite the years of turmoil, the pain, and the scars left by a tumultuous relationship that had spilled over to affect every member of our family, his death unraveled a flood of raw emotion. It was a poignant illustration of the intricate web of feelings that binds us, the way love and hurt can coexist, intertwined in the memories that define our connections to each other.

In the face of Mum's overwhelming despair, the mantle of responsibility fell upon me. The immediacy of death brings with it a cascade of practical necessities—arrangements that wait for no one's grief. I found myself navigating through the motions, a somber checklist that had to be attended to amidst the fog of our collective mourning. Signing for Ray's belongings was a stark, sobering moment. The realisation that all he had left behind, aside from the garments on his back, were the £14 Kevin had recently returned to him, underscored the transient nature of our material existence.

This moment, signing for what little physical evidence remained of Ray's life, was laden with symbolism. It wasn't just the act of retrieving belongings; it was a poignant reflection on what we leave behind, on the legacies—material and emotional—that we impart. The £14, insignificant in monetary value, became a profound testament to the relationships Ray had navigated, a final reminder of the debts we owe each other, not of money, but of love, forgiveness, and the countless small interactions that define a life. In the end, it was these intangible legacies, rather than material possessions, that held the true measure of Ray's impact on our lives.

In the whirlwind that followed Ray's passing, my life became a relentless cycle of obligations. Balancing my full-time job and the ongoing battles with the Council, I now found myself tasked with orchestrating Ray's funeral—a responsibility that consumed every spare moment. The burden of these duties manifested as a tangible weight on my mind, driving me to dedicate an inordinate amount of time and resources to ensuring the funeral reflected the utmost respect for Ray despite our complicated history.

Compelled by a mix of duty and personal expectation, I augmented the modest funeral grant from the council with my own funds. Luxurious black limousines, an array of lavish floral arrangements, and a premium coffin were all chosen in my steadfast commitment to honour Ray with a dignified farewell. This relentless pursuit of perfection in planning the funeral only served to amplify my stress, pushing me to the brink of my endurance. My days blurred into nights with minimal rest, my mind running on an endless loop of funeral details.

The day of the funeral itself was no less hectic. An urgent council meeting concerning Kevin's situation demanded my attention, leaving me to dash home afterwards to don my funeral attire in a frantic rush. Despite the chaos, the service proceeded, and Ray was given a send-off that, I hoped, paid homage to his memory in a manner befitting the complexity of his life.

Afterwards, we gathered at one of Ray's favoured haunts for the wake, a setting familiar with echoes of his presence. It was there, amidst the somber reflections and shared memories, that the pub landlord approached me, perhaps to offer condolences or share a memory of Ray, a moment of human connection in the midst of our collective mourning.

The pub landlord's words caught me off guard, a stark reminder of Ray's turbulent legacy. "Oh, I remember Ray," he remarked with a hint of irony in his tone. "He was actually barred from this pub." In that moment, amidst the solemnity of the wake and the weight of my exhaustive efforts to honour him, the revelation served as a poignant, if somewhat humorous, testament to Ray's character.

Even in death, it seemed, Ray managed to weave a final twist into the narrative of his life, leaving behind a reminder of the complexities and contradictions that had defined him.

The burden of Kevin's precarious living situation still weighed heavily on me, a constant source of stress and heartache that seemed to amplify the challenges of my daily life. In the aftermath of a particularly gruelling encounter with the council, I sought refuge in the familiar act of shopping in Reading town centre. However, the sight of the homeless scattered among the bustling crowds struck a chord deep within me, their presence a stark reminder of the very reality I was fighting so hard to prevent for my brother.

As I navigated through the sea of people, my attention was drawn to one individual in particular. The impulse to extend kindness overwhelmed me, and I found myself pulling £10 from my purse, only to replace it with a £50 note moments later. The palpable sense of isolation and despair emanating from him resonated with me on a profoundly personal level, compelling me to act in the only way I knew how at that moment.

Continuing my journey, I encountered another scene that tugged at my heartstrings: a young homeless man accompanied by a small black dog adorned with a red scarf, a pitiful duo against the backdrop of the slowly falling snow. The young man's disheveled appearance belied his youth, painting a picture of vulnerability that was difficult to ignore. The plight of these two, bracing against the cold with nothing but each other for warmth, filled me with a deep sense of sorrow and helplessness. In them, I saw not just the face of homelessness but a reflection of the fragility of human life, a reminder of the fine line that separates the comfort of home from the harshness of the streets.

Approaching this young man, whom fate had named Kevin like my own brother, I couldn't help but see the parallels between them—a stark reminder of how easily roles could be reversed if not for the support structures we fight to uphold. Engaging in conversation, I found myself not only offering him a meal but also extending a gesture of kindness to his faithful companion. The act of buying them food, a simple yet profound gesture, was my way of acknowledging their struggle and offering a momentary reprieve from their hardships.

In sharing what I had learned from my own battles with the council, I hoped to arm this Kevin with knowledge, perhaps offering him a glimmer of hope or a starting point to navigate the complex maze of social services. The curious glances from passersby did little to deter me; their judgments paled in comparison to the compelling urge I felt to connect and assist.

This encounter profoundly impacted me, rekindling a sense of responsibility not just to my brother but to others facing similar plights. It reinforced my resolve to fight not only for Kevin but for those without a voice or advocate. My subsequent inability to dismiss the appeals of street fundraisers, leading me to support various charities, was a testament to the shift in my perspective. It was a commitment to contribute beyond my immediate circle, influenced by my experiences and the poignant reminder of Hassan's battle with Alzheimer's.

These actions, driven by compassion and a newfound awareness of the interconnectedness of our struggles, were steps towards healing—not just for those I sought to help, but for myself, as I navigated the complexities of grief, responsibility, and the pursuit of justice in a world rife with indifference.

Arriving home to the quiet of 8 Blithe Walk, the act of turning on the TV was meant to be a moment of respite, a brief escape from the whirlwind of emotions and responsibilities that had defined my recent days. Instead, I was confronted with the harrowing images of the Boxing Day tsunami's aftermath. The magnitude of this disaster had slipped past me, unnoticed amid the turmoil of Ray's funeral and the ongoing struggles with Kevin's situation. The scenes unfolding before me—entire landscapes obliterated, families torn apart, survivors grappling with loss—cast a shadow far darker than anything I had encountered in the streets of Reading.

The visceral reaction I had to the suffering of those affected by the tsunami was overwhelming, a profound empathy that seemed to blur the lines between their pain and my own sense of responsibility. This connection, though illogical, felt undeniably real to me in that moment, as if the intensity of my empathy somehow implicated me in their suffering. The guilt that ensued was both irrational and suffocating, a testament to the depth of my compassion but also to the personal turmoil I was experiencing.

Driven by a compulsion to act, to alleviate not just their suffering but the guilt that gnawed at me, I found myself making a substantial donation to the disaster appeal. This act, while a drop in the ocean of need created by such a catastrophic event, was my way of reaching out, of trying to make a difference in the face of helplessness. It was a reflection of a heart stretched thin by personal grief and a broader sorrow for the world's suffering, an attempt to find solace in the act of giving, even as I navigated my own complex web of emotions.

Amidst the turmoil of family challenges and personal grief, my behaviour began to veer into the realm of the erratic, unnoticed by those closest to me. Engulfed in a whirlwind of stress, I found myself seeking solace in the most unconventional ways. The arrival of a random catalogue became the catalyst for a spree of impulsive purchases, culminating in the acquisition of £3,000 worth of unnecessary computer equipment and an assortment of garden gnomes—a stark departure from my usual spending habits. This spree was not just an escape; it was a plunge into a euphoric state, detached from the realities of financial constraints and need.

The extent of my unravelling remained invisible to my family, each member preoccupied with their own struggles. It wasn't until Hassan accompanied me on a trip to town that the first signs of my distress began to surface. My unhesitating act of giving £50 to a homeless person prompted a response from Hassan that revealed his growing concern.

"What on earth are you doing?" Hassan protested.

"I'm just trying to help the homeless," I replied. Hassan shot me a concerned look but said nothing.

The moment I extended a helping hand to the homeless man, his reaction was one of sheer astonishment, intertwined with a deep sense of gratitude. Initially, he seemed not to fully comprehend the magnitude of the gesture, perhaps not recognising at first glance that the piece of paper I had placed into his hand was, in fact, a £50 note. This act of kindness, though simple in its execution, was profound in its impact. As I began to distance myself, moving away from the spot where our paths had crossed, his voice carried over to me, laden with emotion and warmth. "God bless you, ma'am," he called out.

To me, my actions felt wholly justified, a direct expression of my desire to alleviate the suffering around me, even as it betrayed a lack of regard for our own financial stability.

The visit to the Oracle Shopping Centre only intensified these concerns. The vibrant allure of GAP, the clothing store, with its promise of new identities and comforts, propelled me into a frenzy of acquisition. Like a child in a sweet shop, I was driven by a manic energy, indiscriminately adding items to my shopping cart—a vivid illustration of my attempt to fill the voids within me with material goods. This episode, observed by Hassan, marked a turning point, a moment when the hidden turmoil that I had been navigating alone began to spill over into the visible realm, hinting at the need for intervention and support.

"Donna, what are you doing?" asked Hassan, now starting to really worry about me.

Caught in the grip of my own euphoria, the world around me seemed to blur into a backdrop for my frenzied shopping spree. The simple act of selecting clothes transformed into an exhilarating game, each piece a token of momentary joy as I laughed and carelessly flung them into my basket. My actions, though detached from reality, were driven by an overwhelming impulse to accumulate, to seek solace in the tangible while my inner world spun out of control.

As I made my way to the checkout, a seemingly innocuous sight caught my eye: a rail full of clothes outside the dressing room, awaiting their return to the shelves. This minor detail, in the midst of my chaotic joy, suddenly became a beacon of temptation, an invitation to extend my spree even further. It was as if the very fabric of the store conspired to feed into my manic state, offering up endless possibilities for acquisition and the fleeting happiness that came with each new addition to my cart.

"I'll have that too. And that, and that," I said, pointing to garment after garment, to the surprise of the checkout girl.

"Stop. Stop!" cried Hassan. "My wife's sick. She doesn't need all this stuff—she needs an ambulance!"

"It's fine," I told them. "My husband's just under a lot of stress."

In the midst of my shopping frenzy, the store staff observed an odd tableau: me, seemingly just another customer caught up in the joy of retail therapy, and Hassan, visibly distressed by what appeared to be an ordinary situation. To the onlookers, my behaviour might have come off as merely exuberant, rather than a sign of deeper issues at play. This discrepancy between appearance and reality only served to isolate Hassan further, his concern for my well-being misinterpreted as undue alarm.

At this juncture, my ability to mask the turmoil within me was eerily effective. On the surface, I navigated the world with a veneer of normalcy, convincing even myself of my own sanity. My actions, though driven by an underlying psychosis, were cloaked in the semblance of rational choice, making it difficult for anyone, including Hassan and the store staff, to recognise the signs of my distress.

This episode brought out the insidious nature of mental health struggles, where the outward manifestation can often belie the internal chaos. My conviction in my own sanity, despite the burgeoning signs of psychosis, created a chasm between my perception of reality and the actual state of my mental health. Hassan's reaction, steeped in genuine concern, was a stark reminder of the complexities involved in discerning and addressing mental illness, especially in its nascent stages where the line between eccentricity and pathology is perilously thin.

Exasperated, Hassan told me he'd see me at home and left the store. His departure marked the beginning of an even more intense phase of my mania, unfettered by his attempts to ground me in reality. Liberated from his concerned oversight, my senses seemed to amplify, transforming the mall into a kaleidoscope of stimuli. The allure of various scents became a siren call, drawing me irresistibly towards a perfume shop. There, each fragrance sample was not merely a scent but an elixir, offering an intoxicating escape from the tumult within. The experience was transcendent, elevating me to a state of bliss that felt almost otherworldly.

Compelled by this heightened sensory experience, I indulged in a spending spree, purchasing Clinique Happy—a name that seemed to promise the very essence of my ephemeral joy. My next stop was Lush, where I surrounded myself with an array of bath bombs, each one promising an escape into sensory indulgence. In those moments, the financial imprudence of my actions faded into the background, overshadowed by the euphoria of the experience.

This brief interlude of manic happiness, though intensely pleasurable, was a double-edged sword. It offered a stark contrast to the reality waiting for me, a reminder of the precariousness of my mental state. The experience was akin to dancing on the edge of a cliff, reveling in the feeling of liberation even as the ground threatened to give way beneath me. This ecstatic state, accessible only to those who have touched the extremes of human emotion, was a fleeting reprieve from the challenges that lay ahead, a momentary glimpse of happiness in the midst of chaos.

My state of heightened enthusiasm and diminished impulse control made me an ideal target for any salesperson. Driven by a combination of manic energy and a burgeoning religious fervour, I found myself outside Carphone Warehouse. The rationale that propelled me inside was far removed from the practicalities of mobile telecommunications. To me, this wasn't just about upgrading my phone; it was about securing a more direct line to the divine. In my mind, a new phone symbolised a potential lifeline to God, an assurance that when the time came for divine communication, I would be ready and waiting.

This blend of religious conviction and manic optimism continued to dictate my purchases. The next acquisition—a T-shirt emblazoned with "Jesus loves you, but I'm his favourite"—seemed to me not just a whimsical item of clothing but a statement of faith, a tangible expression of my special relationship with the divine. It struck me as the perfect attire for Kevin, imagining it would bring a lighter mood to the serious and often grim proceedings with the council.

As the evening cast its shadow over the Oracle, my departure was accompanied by an intensified sense of divine presence. The simple sight of feathers adrift on the wind captivated me, transforming mundane moments into profound spiritual experiences. These feathers, dancing lightly through the air, seemed to me not mere detritus of the urban landscape but celestial messages, symbols of angelic proximity. This newfound awareness of divine signs enveloped me in a sense of wonder, reinforcing my belief in a personal connection with the divine, a belief that had been both a comfort and a catalyst for my recent actions.

However, this sense of enchantment was quickly overshadowed by the resurgence of a more menacing aspect of my psychosis. The faces of passersby, once just fellow humans navigating their own evening routines, morphed into harbingers of malevolence. Their gazes, which I interpreted through the lens of my heightened paranoia, seemed imbued with sinister intent. This shift from divine euphoria to acute distress was abrupt, turning my journey home into a gauntlet of imagined threats. Reciting the Lord's Prayer became a talisman against the encroaching darkness, a whispered plea for protection and peace in the midst of turmoil.

Upon my frantic arrival at 8 Blithe Walk, the scene that greeted me was one of domestic distress. My mother, enveloped in tears, presented a stark contrast to the spiritual and psychological odyssey I had just endured.

"Donna!" she cried, running to hug me. "Where have you been? We've been looking for you everywhere. We were about to call the police. Hassan left you hours ago and you haven't been answering your phone."

In the stark reality of my living room, surrounded by the tangible evidence of my recent actions, the weight of what I had done began to press down on me. The new phone, purchased in a moment of manic optimism as a supposed direct line to the divine, now seemed a foolish artefact of my delusion. My attempt to reach out to God, encapsulated in a simple text message to a number chosen at random, highlighted the depth of my desperation and confusion.

Surveying the room, the chaos of my purchases sprawled before me—the computer equipment and the whimsical garden gnomes occupying the living space—and served as a physical manifestation of my inner turmoil. Each item, once a symbol of my compulsion to connect, to fill a void, and to seek some form of divine approval, now stood as a testament to the irrationality that had driven me.

The realisation of the financial implications of my actions hit me with full force. The euphoria that had accompanied each purchase, each decision made in the throes of my mania, evaporated, leaving behind a stark sense of guilt and bewilderment. The question of why I had felt compelled to acquire these things, many of which held no practical value or necessity, became a painful reflection of the state I had been in.

As I stood amidst the clutter of my own making, the emotional dam broke. Tears flowed, not just for the money spent but for the recognition of how far I had strayed from reality, how deeply I had been lost in my psychosis.

The looks on my family's faces were unmistakable. "You're not well, Donna," said Mum. "I'm going to call the home treatment team."

As the weight of my recent actions began to suffocate me, Mum became a beacon of patience and care, guiding me to a place of temporary peace. Her act of tucking me into bed with a warm cup of tea was a gentle reminder of the enduring presence of love amidst chaos. My mind, however, remained ensnared by a tumult of spiritual questions and visions, seeking answers about the divine and the afterlife—a reflection of my desperate search for solace and understanding. The vivid imagery of heaven that danced before my eyes, with its promise of respite and purity, became a focal point of my longing, a beacon of hope in the midst of my turmoil.

The intervention of the home treatment team that evening, marked by the administration of a sedative, was a turning point. It brought with it the first semblance of real rest I had experienced in what felt like an eternity, a brief hiatus from the relentless grip of my manic episode. The arrival of the doctor the next morning signified the beginning of a new chapter in my journey towards healing.

"Please," I begged. "Don't send me back to the hospital."

But my husband thought otherwise. "I think she needs to be taken away," he said.

Hearing Hassan's words left me devastated, torn between the shame of a potential return to Prospect Park Psychiatric Hospital and the fear of my colleagues discovering my condition. Despite this, my illness was undeniable, manifesting vividly as I experienced hallucinations of objects moving around the room while the doctor spoke. After consenting to take my antipsychotic medication, the doctor consented to my being treated at home. Over the next two weeks, a fierce struggle ensued between the medication and my psychosis, until slowly, the intensity of my mania began to decrease, akin to the gradual lowering of a thermostat's dial.

Following the intense mania, the inevitable descent into depression was harsh and unrelenting. The aftermath of such highs always comes with a profound low, and this time was no exception. Daily routines and simple activities became Herculean tasks, each day a battle against the inertia that the depression cast over me.

The visit to Erleigh Road Clinic brought with it a new, sobering diagnosis: bipolar disorder. This wasn't just another episode; it was an acknowledgment of a long-term battle with a condition that demanded constant vigilance and management. The realisation that my mental health struggles were not isolated incidents but part of a lifelong journey was a heavy burden to bear.

Yet, amidst the turmoil, I found a sliver of hope in the prospect of returning to work. After four months of wrestling with my diagnosis and its implications, I pushed myself to re-enter the workforce at the Prudential. I rationalised that my absence, this time framed as a bereavement leave rather than a psychiatric hospitalisation, would attract less scrutiny and gossip among my colleagues. This decision to return to work was not just about reclaiming a sense of normalcy; it was an act of defiance against the condition that sought to define me, a step towards regaining control over my life and narrative.

Navigating the reality of my own long-term mental health condition paralleled the journey I was on with Hassan, each of us locked in our own battles yet united in our search for clarity and hope. Despite the weight of my diagnosis, my determination to understand and improve Hassan's condition never waned. We traversed the landscape of medical opinions, subjecting him to a battery of tests that ranged from wearing wires for brainwave monitoring to undergoing numerous MRI scans, all in the quest for answers.

The referral to a renowned neurologist in London marked a pivotal moment in this journey. Her review of Hassan's extensive medical investigations brought with it a revelation that shifted the ground beneath our feet. The letter from her, once opened, transformed our outlook in ways we hadn't dared to hope for. The diagnosis we had braced ourselves to confront head-on— Alzheimer's—was not the spectre looming over us. Instead, she proposed that the intense stress and preoccupation with his legal battle had manifested in a profound, yet fundamentally different, impact on his cognitive health.

This unexpected turn in Hassan's diagnosis, devoid of the degenerative and terminal implications of Alzheimer's, opened up a new realm of possibilities and challenges. While it spared us the grim trajectory we had anticipated, it also underscored the intricate and often underestimated interplay between mental and emotional stress and physical health. The revelation was a double-edged sword, offering relief from one fear while presenting a complex array of psychological and neurological effects to understand and address.

The news that Hassan's condition was not the terminal sentence we had feared brought a profound sense of relief. The grim future I had envisioned, one of loss and suffering, was suddenly replaced with hope. The thought that we still had the opportunity to share our lives together, albeit altered by the trials we had faced, was a beacon of light in the turmoil that had engulfed us.

However, this relief was swiftly overshadowed by a surge of anger and betrayal. The initial misdiagnosis that had thrown our lives into chaos now seemed like a cruel twist of fate. My descent into psychosis, spurred by the overwhelming fear and despair of losing Hassan, had been a reaction to a reality that was never ours to face.

The consequences of that period—a lingering vulnerability to stress and the onset of a lifelong mental health condition—were burdens I would now carry indefinitely. This realisation that my own health had been compromised, potentially needlessly, due to a diagnostic error, ignited a sense of injustice.

The irony of the situation was not lost on me. In seeking to support and care for Hassan, I had unwittingly stepped into a maelanotic spiral that not only threatened my own life but also fundamentally altered the trajectory of my health and well-being. The path that lay ahead, marked by the need for constant vigilance against the shadows of further relapses, was a stark reminder of the fragility of our attempts to control our destinies. Life, with its unpredictable twists and the profound impact of human error, had dealt a hand that was indeed impossibly cruel, leaving us to navigate the aftermath as best we could.

Chapter Nine

The Episode

Life at 8 Blithe Walk resumed its rhythm, a semblance of normalcy woven from the threads of routine and resignation. Amidst the backdrop of a home saturated with the echoes of past tumults, including the stark memories of my own battles with psychosis, I found a measure of stability in the mundane tasks of daily life. Working full-time and managing the household chores over the weekends became my new normal, especially as Mum's arthritis worsened, limiting her ability to contribute.

The spectre of my mental health condition loomed large, yet, with diligent adherence to my treatment plan, I managed to keep the demons at bay. The fear of becoming a "revolving-door patient", caught in a cycle of hospital admissions and discharges, gradually receded as the months rolled into years without incident. This achievement, however, came at a cost. The reflection that greeted me in the mirror bore little resemblance to the woman I once knew. The side effects of my medication had exacted a heavy toll on my physical appearance, transforming me in ways that felt alien and unwelcome.

Confronted with the visual reminder of this transformation each day, a growing sense of discontent took root within me. The medication, while a lifeline, had also become a symbol of my loss of self, a daily marker of the ways in which my condition had reshaped my identity. It was in this moment of reflection, faced with the tangible evidence of the trade-offs between mental stability and physical change, that I reached a breaking point. The decision to stop taking my medication was borne from a deep desire to reclaim a part of myself that felt lost, a desperate bid to reconnect with the person I used to be before the onset of my illness and its ensuing consequences. This choice, fraught with risk and longing, was a testament to the complex and often painful negotiations we make in the pursuit of wellness and self-recognition.

During my routine psychiatric review, I found myself confessing to my psychiatrist that I had ceased taking my medication. His response was immediate and grave, outlining the stark consequences of my decision: "Donna, the medication will keep you well. If you don't take it, you'll have more relapses, and each time, they'll get worse." His warning was rooted in a deep understanding of the nature of bipolar disorder and the critical role that medication plays in managing the condition. Despite his cautionary advice, my resolve remained unshaken.

Empowered by a fleeting sense of well-being and the visible results of my weight loss, I stood firm in my decision. The brief hiatus from the side effects of the medication had reintroduced me to aspects of myself that I had long missed, bolstering my belief that I could maintain my mental health without pharmaceutical intervention. This conviction, however strong, overlooked the complex and often unpredictable nature of mental illness, setting the stage for a potentially perilous gamble with my well-being.

Navigating through the year without my medication, I found a semblance of stability that allowed me to focus on my goals. The pursuit of my diploma in financial planning became a beacon of hope, a tangible step towards a future that promised not only a career advancement but also a potential escape from the confines of 8 Blithe Walk. The prospect of achieving this milestone invigorated me, offering a clear path towards improving our financial situation and, ultimately, our living conditions.

However, this period was also marked by significant professional challenges. A major project at work, centred on the complex task of redistributing an inherited estate, demanded my full engagement. My role as a technical advisor placed me at the heart of this intricate process, compelling me to extend my working hours well beyond the norm. The commitment to excellence that had always guided my work ethic led me to sacrifice my weekends in the pursuit of perfection, a testament to my determination to contribute meaningfully to the project's success.

Additionally, the opportunity to contribute an article to the company magazine added another layer of responsibility to my already crowded schedule. My evenings, once reserved for rest and personal time, were now occupied with research and writing, further blurring the lines between my professional and personal lives. This intense period of work, while a reflection of my commitment and ambition, also underscored the delicate balance between pursuing career aspirations and maintaining mental and physical well-being.

The physical strain of my demanding schedule began manifesting in troubling symptoms, prompting a visit to the optician. The diagnosis of potential migraines and the prescription of glasses for computer work were tangible signs that the intense focus on my professional responsibilities was taking a toll on my health. My failure to collect the prescribed glasses due to extended work hours was a clear indication of how consumed I had become by my job.

The realisation that I had forgotten Hassan's birthday in the whirlwind of my commitments was a heart-wrenching moment. Racing home, burdened with guilt over my oversight, I discovered Hassan, unaffected by the date, a poignant reminder of the challenges we faced together. The mix of love, guilt, and exhaustion overwhelmed me, bringing into sharp relief the extent to which work had begun to overshadow the most important aspects of my life.

This moment of clarity amidst the chaos of my professional and personal obligations was a wake-up call. It underscored the necessity of finding a balance, of recognising when the pursuit of career goals and the accumulation of stress begin to detrimentally impact health and relationships. It was a stark reminder of the need to prioritise well-being and the value of the moments we share with loved ones, amidst the relentless demands of life.

Ignoring the mounting stress and the missed warning signs, I was propelled into a state of crisis far quicker than I had anticipated. The initial physical symptoms, a peculiar tingling that escalated into an unbearable heat, were merely the precursors to a more profound psychological unraveling. My perception of my surroundings became distorted, marked by a return of the terrifying hallucinations that characterised my previous episodes of psychosis. The innocuous glance from a colleague morphed in my mind into a manifestation of malevolence, reigniting the paralysing fear and mistrust I had fought so hard to overcome.

Seeking refuge in the solitude of a bathroom cubicle, I found myself overwhelmed by a sense of impending doom. The physical discomfort was compounded by a psychological torment, leaving me isolated and afraid in a place that had once felt familiar and safe. Despite my attempts to regain composure, the journey back to my desk was a gauntlet of perceived threats, each colleague's gaze seeming to conceal sinister intentions.

Compelled by a desperate need to alert someone to the danger I believed was imminent, I reached out to my boss via email, a modern-day cry for help. This act, driven by a distorted perception of reality, was a clear indication that the delicate balance I had strived to maintain had been shattered, leaving me once again at the mercy of my own mind.

I've seen it, I wrote enigmatically, and it's everywhere.

In a familiar pattern, my delusions once again shifted, this time from fear to overwhelming love and gratitude towards those around me. Driven by a sense of duty to acknowledge their efforts, I embarked on a mission to express my appreciation by printing off reward certificates for each member of my team. Despite the puzzled glances exchanged among my colleagues, I remained undeterred, convinced that these gestures of gratitude were a potent antidote to the perceived malevolence encircling me.

With each certificate bestowed, a sense of relief washed over me, alleviating the searing discomfort that had plagued me throughout the day. Buoyed by these acts of kindness, I left the office enveloped in a euphoric haze, my spirits soaring to new heights. As I stepped into the tumultuous weather outside, a surreal moment unfolded, with the hail serving as a stark contrast to the sudden break in the clouds. Bathed in a shaft of sunlight, I felt an undeniable sense of divine presence, a conviction that I was now working in service of a higher purpose.

As Hassan's daughter, Leila, prepared to visit from Dublin that evening, I found myself consumed by a frantic urge to tidy the house in anticipation of her arrival. However, a peculiar compulsion overtook me, compelling me to adorn the living room with pictures of Che Guevara, plastering them across every available surface.

Long after the rest of the household had retired for the night, I remained in the living room, where I had taken to sleeping. There, amidst fits of laughter and tears, I grappled with an overwhelming conviction that a monumental conflict loomed on the horizon, and inexplicably, I alone bore the burden of this foreknowledge. The weight of this perceived responsibility bore down on me relentlessly, threatening to engulf me entirely.

Terrified and disoriented, I dashed into the kitchen only to be confronted by a ghastly sight: a shrouded figure lying motionless on the floor, unmistakably resembling Hassan. Fear gripped me as I hesitated to uncover the body, paralysed by the dread of confirming my worst fears. Yet, before I could muster the courage, I fled back into the living room, where a bewildering scene awaited me: Hassan, alive and well, stood before me.

Caught in the throes of confusion and paranoia, I struggled to discern reality from hallucination, uncertain whether the Hassan in front of me was genuine or merely a figment of my tortured mind.

My husband looked around the room, taking in the pictures of Che pinned to every wall. "What's going on, Donna?" he asked gently. He tried to smile reassuringly, but his attempt at reassurance felt hollow, his smile appearing sinister in my deluded state. Desperate for solace, I clandestinely retrieved my old crucifix, clutching it tightly behind my back as I whispered the Lord's Prayer, seeking protection from the malevolent forces I believed surrounded me.

Hassan promptly summoned my mother, who recognised the telltale signs of another episode unfolding. She wasted no time in contacting the crisis line, and before I knew it, I was hurriedly packing my suitcase, preparing for yet another stint at Prospect Park Psychiatric Hospital. Despite the gravity of the situation, I felt strangely detached, unable to comprehend the reality of my circumstances. In my bewildered state, I mindlessly stuffed my case with books, Che Guevara T-shirts, and my wedding album, the gravity of the situation eluding me.

"Maybe you should put some underwear and things in, Donna?" Leila suggested, sensing my confusion, prompting me to comply like a child. As we waited in the hospital reception, my hallucinations persisted, distorting my perception of reality beyond recognition. The faces of loved ones morphed into demonic visages before my eyes, confirming the doctor's grim prognosis: I had irrevocably lost touch with reality. Upon admission, I collapsed to the ground in despair, tears flowing freely as I grappled with the overwhelming dread of impending calamity.

Within the confines of the TV lounge, I found no respite from my torment. Every image, every face, seemed to exude malevolence, fuelling my conviction that the world was in the grip of sinister forces. As I sat helplessly on the sofa, a sinister spectre materialised before me, encircling me in a sinister dance of malice. Paralysed with terror, I succumbed to unconsciousness, my mind a battleground between delusion and despair.

As consciousness slowly reclaimed me, an urgent sense of purpose surged within. Convinced of my divine mission to avert the impending catastrophe, I felt compelled to leave the confines of the hospital without a moment's hesitation. Ignoring the necessity of gathering my belongings, I made a beeline for the exit, driven by an unwavering resolve to fulfill what I believed to be my sacred duty.

"Where are you going?" asked one of the nurses.

"I've got to go," I replied. "Can you open the door, please?"

"I don't think that's a good idea, Donna," she replied.

In a frenzied state of desperation, I gazed up at the wall, fixating on the fire alarm encased within its glass barrier. Without a second thought, I thrust my hand forward, shattering the protective casing and triggering the piercing wail of the alarm. Amidst the ensuing pandemonium, I seized the opportunity to bolt for the exit, driven by a primal instinct to escape. Yet, my bid for freedom was short-lived as additional staff swiftly intervened, administering sedatives to quell my tumultuous frenzy. When I regained consciousness, I was confronted with the grim reality: I had been involuntarily detained under mental health legislation. With a heavy heart, I realised that in addition to losing my grip on sanity, I had now forfeited my autonomy, ensnared within the confines of institutional confinement.

The tranquillising effects of the medication gradually subdued the harrowing illusions that had plagued my mind, but the stark reality of life within the hospital proved to be anything but serene. Placed once again on Daisy Ward, the very unit I had previously discharged myself from due to its pervasive drug culture and intimidating atmosphere, I found myself navigating a tense and unsettling environment.

One fateful day, as I traversed the corridor, I encountered a distressed young female patient. Clad solely in her nightdress and barefoot, her body bore the unmistakable signs of bruising, prompting unsettling suspicions of potential abuse. Without warning, she launched herself at me with an overwhelming fury, viciously tearing my glasses from my face and hurling them to the ground before mercilessly stomping on them. In a frenzied frenzy, she screamed and raged, her wild gestures and frantic attempts to harm me leaving me shaken and profoundly unsettled. Amidst the chaos, hospital staff swiftly intervened to restrain her, yet her primal aggression lingered, casting a pall of fear and unease over the ward.

The abrupt assault left me trembling with confusion and a deep sense of unease. Struggling to comprehend what might have incited such a violent outburst, my mind raced with conjectures, settling upon the haunting possibility that my mere presence, marked by the glasses that had unwittingly become a catalyst for trauma, had triggered the young girl's distressing reaction.

Despite the unsettling incident, I sought solace and companionship among the other patients on the ward, forming bonds with souls whose struggles mirrored and, in some cases, surpassed my own. Among them was a young man grappling with addiction, bearing a striking resemblance to my brother, Kevin. His ravaged appearance bore witness to the toll of his substance abuse, his once vibrant youth eclipsed by the harsh realities of neglect and addiction. Moved by empathy and a sense of kinship, I assumed a nurturing role, offering him guidance and support amidst the tumult of our shared experiences, finding a semblance of solace in the act of caring for another amidst the chaos of my own turmoil.

The news of my release from being sectioned brought a mix of emotions. Relief washed over me, yet it was tinged with a bitter acknowledgment of how dire my situation had become. The label of having been sectioned now marked me permanently, a stark reminder of the depths to which my mental health had plunged.

As I gradually reintegrated into periods of leave, returning home for brief respites from the confines of the hospital, I found no solace in the semblance of normalcy it offered. The overcrowded house remained unchanged, with my makeshift living arrangements in the living room serving as a constant reminder of my fractured sense of belonging. Amidst the chaos of familial struggles, from my husband's health concerns to my brother's addiction and my own battles with depression, I grappled with a profound sense of displacement, unsure whether the familiarity of home or the structured confines of the hospital were the lesser of two evils.

Chapter Ten

The Return

Eventually, I had no choice but to return to 8 Blithe Walk for good. The realisation that I could never return to work hit me like a ton of bricks. Despite my years of dedication and hard work, my career aspirations were abruptly dashed by the harsh reality of my bipolar disorder. The doctor's verdict was clear: returning to work posed too great a risk to my fragile mental health, and the only path forward was a life of reduced stress and lifelong medication.

It was a devastating blow. All the effort I had poured into completing my exams and pursuing my dream of becoming a financial advisor felt futile. My hard-earned qualifications now seemed nothing more than meaningless pieces of paper. However, the silver lining was the continued support from Prudential, which ensured a percentage of my wage, providing some semblance of financial stability amidst the wreckage of shattered ambitions.

With each successive relapse, the toll on my mental health grew heavier. The periods of depression that followed my manic episodes seemed to deepen, leaving me feeling more fragile and unstable each time I attempted to return to normalcy. Work had always been a lifeline for both Mum and me, providing structure, purpose, and a sense of security. Now, faced with empty days devoid of the familiar routine of employment, I found myself adrift in a sea of mundane household tasks.

Meanwhile, Mum continued to toil away at her full-time job despite her declining health and worsening arthritis. The added burden of a mild cognitive impairment diagnosis only added to the weight on my shoulders. After witnessing Hassan's decline, the news hit me like a sledgehammer. I could only pray that Mum's condition wouldn't progress further, yet a nagging sense of foreboding lingered, as if our family were cursed with an unending streak of misfortune.

In my 40s, the harsh reality sank in: the window for me to ever experience motherhood had closed shut. I had clung to the hope of one day cradling a child of my own, a chance to fill the void left by the one I had relinquished with Tony. Yet, the medications that had become my lifeline over the years were now a barrier to conception. After the harrowing experience of attempting to manage without them, only to spiral into another episode, I had little choice but to heed the doctor's counsel and resign myself to a lifetime of medication.

The weight of this realisation pressed heavily upon me, casting a shadow over my dreams of a family. Each passing year seemed to reinforce the sense of loss, reminding me of the fleeting nature of time and the choices I had made. While I had once imagined the patter of tiny feet and the joy of motherhood, those aspirations now felt like distant echoes of a life I could never fully embrace.

Amidst this bittersweet acknowledgment, one beacon of joy remained: Hassan's daughter, Leila. With her long, dark hair and piercing green eyes, she had blossomed into a radiant young woman. Her remarkable talent as a singer brought light into our lives, a reminder of hope and beauty amidst the struggles we faced. Leila's presence filled our home with warmth and vitality, offering solace in the face of our shared challenges and reminding us of the power of love to transcend even the darkest of times.

After two years of receiving part-pay due to my redundancy from the Prudential, a significant payout finally landed in my bank account. It was a sudden influx of funds, a financial windfall that seemed to breathe new life into our stagnant circumstances. For the first time in years, I found myself with a surplus of money, a rare and precious commodity in our household.

Inspired by the transformative experience of my trip to London, I resolved to seize this opportunity to create something extraordinary for our family. With a sense of determination and hope, I took decisive action and booked a trip to Israel for Hassan and myself. It was a journey fuelled by the desire to reconnect Hassan with his family's ancestral lands in Palestine, to revisit the place that held such profound significance in his heritage.

As we ventured into the heart of Palestine, the landscape unfolded before us, a tapestry of history and memory intertwined. We found ourselves standing in the vicinity of the house that once belonged to Hassan's parents before the upheavals of war altered the course of their lives. The emotions were palpable as we gazed upon the structure, a tangible link to Hassan's past.

However, our moment of reflection was abruptly interrupted when the current occupants emerged, their voices raised in anger and hostility. We were swiftly escorted away by the authorities, our encounter tinged with tension and apprehension. Yet, despite the harrowing experience, I could sense the profound impact it had on Hassan. His eyes reflected a mixture of nostalgia and gratitude, a testament to the significance of our journey.

Though our visit was fraught with challenges, it was a poignant reminder of the enduring power of heritage and the resilience of the human spirit. Despite the obstacles we faced, Hassan's sense of belonging and connection to his roots remained steadfast, a testament to the enduring bond between identity and homeland.

Back in the familiar surroundings of Reading, I found myself contemplating the trajectory of my life, searching for avenues that could infuse my existence with a deeper sense of purpose. The doctor's cautionary words lingered in my mind, a constant reminder of the fragile balance I now navigated. The spectre of relapse loomed large, each episode eroding my memory and leaving behind a trail of fear and uncertainty.

Yet, amid the apprehension, a glimmer of possibility emerged. Perhaps, within the confines of my limitations, there existed opportunities to engage with the community, to carve out a semblance of routine and connection that had eluded me in recent years.

With a newfound sense of determination, I embarked on a journey of volunteering, seeking solace and fulfilment in service to others. At a quaint café nestled by the tranquil banks of the river, I found my sanctuary, a haven for individuals grappling with their own mental health challenges. My role was simple yet profoundly rewarding: serving tea, cake, and sandwiches with a warmth and compassion born from shared experience.

Though the patrons of the café remained unaware of my personal struggles, there existed an unspoken bond, a silent understanding that transcended words. In their eyes, I recognised reflections of my own journey—a testament to the universal nature of human suffering and resilience. These were not merely individuals shunned by society's indifference, but kindred spirits, seeking solace and acceptance in a world fraught with misunderstanding.

As I immersed myself in conversations and shared moments of camaraderie, a realisation dawned upon me: perhaps, amidst the chaos and turmoil of my own life, I had acquired a precious gift. My experiences, though marred by hardship, had bestowed upon me a reservoir of empathy and understanding, a currency with which to navigate the labyrinth of human suffering.

With each interaction, I discovered the transformative power of empathy, the ability to offer solace and companionship to those traversing similar paths. In the quiet moments of reflection, I began to discern a profound truth: that amidst the wreckage of my own struggles, lay the seeds of redemption, the promise of a life dedicated to service and compassion.

The doctors' prognosis had been bleak, their expectations of my future confined by the boundaries of my diagnosis. Yet, with each passing day, I defied their predictions, finding solace and strength in pursuits that nourished my spirit rather than jeopardising my mental well-being. The realisation dawned upon me with a quiet certainty: I was capable of contributing meaningfully to the world, of making a difference that transcended the confines of my illness.

My journey through the labyrinth of mental health had endowed me with a wealth of knowledge and insight, a tapestry woven from personal experiences and the wisdom gleaned from countless books and resources. The intricacies of the human mind, once shrouded in mystery, had become a familiar landscape, navigated with a sense of familiarity and understanding.

Yet, the path forward remained veiled in uncertainty. How could I transition from my past life of office work, now distant and estranged, to a realm where my newfound expertise could find expression? The ravages of illness had eroded my confidence, leaving behind a shadow of doubt that lingered with each tentative step.

Simple tasks that once held no challenge now loomed dauntingly before me, a testament to the toll exacted by my illness. Even the prospect of using a computer, once a familiar tool in my arsenal, now evoked a sense of trepidation and uncertainty.

Yet, amidst the uncertainty, a flicker of determination ignited within me. I refused to be confined by the limitations imposed upon me, to relinquish the possibility of a future where my experiences could serve as a beacon of hope for others traversing similar paths. The journey ahead would be arduous, fraught with challenges and setbacks, but within the depths of my soul burned a steadfast resolve to reclaim my agency, to forge a new path guided by compassion and purpose.

With a renewed sense of purpose, I embarked on a journey of self-improvement, determined to bridge the gap between my past and the possibilities of the future. Refresher courses in office skills became my stepping stones, guiding me back to familiarity with programs like Word and Excel, each keystroke a testament to my resilience and determination. As I delved deeper, my efforts culminated in the attainment of a diploma in office skills, a tangible symbol of my perseverance and dedication.

Armed with newfound confidence and qualifications, I eagerly scoured the job listings on the NHS website, a beacon of opportunity in the realm of mental health care. Then, like a beacon in the night, it appeared—a vacancy for a ward clerk at Prospect Park Psychiatric Hospital, a place synonymous with both my struggles and my journey towards healing. Despite its modest stature compared to my previous role at Prudential, the significance of this opportunity transcended mere job titles and responsibilities.

For me, this position represented more than just employment; it was a chance to make a tangible difference in the lives of those who, like me, had traversed the labyrinth of mental illness. No longer driven by aspirations of status or prestige, my focus had shifted towards pursuits that resonated with the essence of my journey: compassion, empathy, and a shared understanding of adversity.

Though the role may have been menial in the eyes of some, its potential for impact was immeasurable. It offered me a foothold in the realm of mental health care, an opportunity to explore the myriad roles and responsibilities that awaited, and a chance to contribute to a cause greater than myself. As I prepared to embark on this new chapter, I did so with a sense of anticipation, eager to discover the depths of possibility that lay before me.

As I sat in the familiar reception area, awaiting my interview, a wave of apprehension washed over me. Memories of past visits to this building resurfaced, each one a reminder of the tumultuous journey I had endured. The same corridors, the same reception desk—it was as if time had stood still, frozen in the moments of my darkest struggles.

In the midst of my unease, I found solace in the knowledge that I had every right to be there. Despite the ghosts of my past haunting the hallways, I was determined to confront them head-on, armed with the courage born from resilience and determination. My decision to disclose my medical history on the HR forms was a testament to my commitment to transparency, a bold declaration of my willingness to embrace my past as part of my journey forward.

As the minutes ticked by, I reminded myself of the stakes at hand. What did I have to lose? This opportunity represented more than just a job interview; it was a chance to reclaim my sense of purpose, to redefine my identity beyond the confines of illness. With each passing moment, my nerves gave way to a quiet resolve, a steadfast determination to seize the moment and carve out a future filled with hope and possibility.

The news of securing the job filled me with an overwhelming sense of accomplishment and relief. It was as if a weight had been lifted off my shoulders, and I could finally see a path forward, illuminated by newfound hope and purpose. As I shared the news with my psychiatrist, his reassurance and support bolstered my confidence, reaffirming my decision to embark on this new chapter of my life.

Transitioning into my role at the mental health intensive care ward felt like stepping into a realm of possibility and opportunity. The unfamiliar faces and surroundings provided a sense of anonymity, allowing me to embrace my fresh start with a renewed sense of optimism. Guided by the warmth and hospitality of the deputy ward manager, I quickly acclimated to my surroundings, immersing myself in the tasks at hand with a sense of determination and enthusiasm.

With each passing day, I found myself settling into a rhythm, relishing in the structure and routine that my job provided. The once daunting prospect of empty days ahead now gave way to a sense of purpose and fulfilment, as I immersed myself in the meaningful work of supporting others on their journey towards recovery. While the financial rewards may not have matched those of my previous career, the sense of fulfilment and contentment I derived from my new role far outweighed any material gains.

In embracing this new chapter of my life, I rediscovered a sense of identity and resilience that had long lay dormant within me. With each passing day, I felt a little more like my old self, empowered by the knowledge that I was making a difference in the lives of others while reclaiming control over my own destiny.

Interacting with the patients became the highlight of my day, bringing a sense of fulfillment and purpose that transcended any professional accolades or career advancements. Positioned by the door to the communal area, I became a familiar face to those seeking assistance or simply a friendly conversation. Whether it was fetching an extra towel or retrieving an item from their locker, I welcomed every opportunity to engage with the patients, offering a listening ear and a compassionate presence.

In addition to my administrative duties, I eagerly volunteered to assist with the music therapy group, recognising the therapeutic value of creative expression in the healing process. Through these activities, I began to forge genuine connections with the patients, getting to know them as individuals with unique stories and struggles.

One such individual was Charlie, a man navigating his own journey with bipolar disorder. Despite occasional displays of unintentional aggression, I made a concerted effort to extend kindness and understanding towards him, ensuring he felt valued and included within the community. From delivering his morning paper to donating specialised socks for his swollen leg, I sought to alleviate his discomfort and foster a sense of dignity in the midst of adversity.

It was heartening to witness the transformative power of small gestures of kindness, knowing that even amidst the clinical setting of a hospital, human connection could serve as a beacon of hope and compassion. Thus, when Charlie sought my support as a chaperone for a crucial meeting with his doctors, I was deeply moved by his trust and gratitude, reaffirming the profound impact of empathy and solidarity in the journey towards healing and recovery.

Edward, a young man grappling with the tumult of mania, often sought solace in our conversations. Knocking on my door, he would pour out his heart, expressing profound shame at his hospitalisation and a sense of hopelessness about the future. As he shared his innermost struggles, I offered a listening ear and words of reassurance, gently reminding him that his current circumstances did not define his worth. I emphasised the hospital as a place of healing and growth, assuring him that brighter days lay ahead on his journey to recovery.

Each interaction with Edward was a poignant reminder of the resilience and vulnerability inherent in the human experience. Sitting by his side, I witnessed the raw intensity of his emotions and the weight of societal stigma bearing down upon him. Yet, amidst his despair, there flickered a glimmer of hope—a belief in the possibility of redemption and renewal.

As patients bid farewell to the ward, they left behind tokens of gratitude in the form of heartfelt letters and cards. These expressions of appreciation served as a testament to the impact of our connections and the significance of empathy in the realm of mental health care. Though the financial rewards of my previous career were substantial, the intrinsic value of these gestures far surpassed any monetary measure. Each letter was a testament to the profound impact of compassion and companionship, reinforcing my conviction in the power of human connection to foster healing and resilience.

A decade has passed since my last relapse, marking a transformative journey of self-discovery and resilience. Through trial and tribulation, I've gained invaluable insights into managing my mental health, recognising the significance of medication as a lifelong companion on my path to stability. While the prospect of a high-powered career in finance may have dimmed, I've come to embrace a different path—one defined by compassion, purpose, and service to others.

In navigating the complexities of my condition, I've cultivated a profound acceptance of my reality, embracing the notion that true fulfilment lies not in societal accolades or material success, but in the simple yet profound act of nurturing the well-being of those around me. My journey has led me to redefine success, shifting my focus from external achievements to the cultivation of inner peace and connection.

Amidst the ebb and flow of life's challenges, I've discovered a sense of purpose in caring for others, recognising the profound impact of empathy and support in the realm of mental health. Whether it's through my role as a caregiver, volunteer, or advocate, I've found solace in the knowledge that every act of kindness, no matter how small, has the power to ignite hope and healing in the lives of those I touch.

As I reflect on my journey, I'm filled with gratitude for the resilience and strength that have carried me through the darkest of times. While the road ahead may be uncertain, I navigate it with a sense of courage and determination, knowing that my experiences have equipped me with the wisdom and resilience to face whatever challenges may arise. And in embracing this newfound sense of purpose and fulfilment, I've discovered a profound sense of peace and contentment that transcends the limitations of my past aspirations.

Over the years, I've come to understand that managing stress is paramount in safeguarding my mental well-being—a lifelong commitment that requires a multifaceted approach. From the soothing embrace of yoga to the invigorating release of exercise, I've cultivated a toolkit of strategies aimed at mitigating the effects of stress and maintaining equilibrium in the face of life's challenges.

My arsenal includes an array of comforting rituals and sensory delights, from lavender neck pillows to the soft glow of mood lighting, each carefully chosen to soothe the mind and nurture the spirit. Bath oils and relaxation tapes offer a sanctuary of tranquillity, providing moments of respite amidst the chaos of daily life.

Central to my approach is a comprehensive plan for managing stress, meticulously documented in a pack at home. This resource serves as a roadmap, outlining warning signs and offering a repertoire of coping mechanisms to deploy when stress threatens to overwhelm. From the subtle pressure behind the eyes to the restless nights and heightened perceptions, I've learned to heed these signals as guideposts on the path to self-care.

While the journey may be marked by familiar challenges and moments of uncertainty, I've come to recognise the power of self-awareness and resilience in navigating the complexities of bipolar disorder. It's a journey of empowerment—one where I refuse to let the diagnosis define me, but instead, harness its lessons to cultivate a life of balance, purpose, and fulfilment. With dedication and perseverance, I've discovered that living with bipolar disorder is not a sentence of defeat, but an opportunity for growth, resilience, and self-discovery.

Seven years ago marked a significant chapter in our lives as Mum made the decision to sell 8 Blithe Walk, the home we had known for so many years. It was a bittersweet moment, bidding farewell to the place where countless memories had been woven into the fabric of our lives. Mum had purchased the house under the Right to Buy scheme, and with the proceeds from its sale, coupled with my redundancy pay out, we embarked on a new chapter, purchasing a spacious four-bedroom bungalow nestled on the outskirts of Reading.

Our new abode offered a sanctuary of tranquillity, boasting a quarter-acre garden adorned with a delightful array of features. A charming patio provided the perfect spot for al fresco gatherings, while a serene goldfish pond added a touch of serenity to the landscape. Towering above it all stood a majestic oak tree, its sprawling branches casting a comforting shade over the lush greenery. Amidst this idyllic setting, a small bench served as a poignant tribute to my beloved brother Mark, whose memory we cherished dearly and whose presence lingered in our hearts.

As the years unfolded, both Hassan and Mum continued to grapple with bouts of forgetfulness, yet mercifully, neither succumbed to the ravages of Alzheimer's disease. When we humorously commented on Hassan's forgetfulness, I playfully described it as him having "mad professor syndrome".Mum, resilient as ever, defied the odds, persevering in her work endeavours well into her later years. Despite undergoing two hip replacements, she remained steadfast in her commitment, retiring only when she turned 76. Even now, at the remarkable age of 83, Mum continues to exude vitality and resilience, a testament to her unwavering spirit and indomitable resolve.

On lazy weekends, the three of us, Hassan, Mum, and I, would find solace in the tranquillity of our garden oasis. As the golden hues of the setting sun paint the sky, we'd gather together, each with a drink in hand, cherishing the simple pleasures of togetherness. Our beloved feline companion, Smokey, frolicking playfully across the emerald expanse of the lawn, her antics adding a touch of whimsy to our idyllic scene.

The transition from the confines of 8 Blithe Walk to our new abode had been nothing short of transformative, liberating us from the shadows of the past and ushering in a renewed sense of hope and optimism. No longer tethered to the painful memories that once haunted us, we now stood on the threshold of a promising future, brimming with anticipation for the adventures that lay ahead.

In this sanctuary of serenity, surrounded by the lush beauty of nature, we found respite from the turbulence of life's trials and tribulations. Here, amidst the gentle rustle of leaves and the melodious chirping of birds, we rediscovered the joy of simply being together, savouring each precious moment as it unfolded.

As we basked in the glow of twilight, our hearts were filled with gratitude for the journey that had brought us to this moment. With hopeful hearts and unwavering resolve, we eagerly embraced the possibilities that the future holds, united in our shared vision of a life filled with love, laughter, and boundless happiness.

Chapter Eleven

The Christmas

On Christmas Day of 2016, a day that marked our first holiday season in our new home, the gravity of Mark's illness became unmistakably clear to me. Christmas was a time of joy for Mark, and it was profoundly unsettling to witness him too ill to join us at the dining table, a place where he customarily revelled in the festive atmosphere. Despite my efforts to prepare a Christmas feast with all the traditional trimmings for the family, Mark's absence was a stark and worrisome sign.

The dining table was elegantly dressed in a festive tablecloth of red, cream, and green, reserved exclusively for this cherished celebration. As the eldest, Mark's designated seat was at the head of the table, a place of honour opposite to where our mother sat. A beautiful garland of green pine, adorned with white candles and acorns, stretched down the centre of the table, complemented by red placemats and decorative Christmas crackers that lay beside the sparkling wine glasses, awaiting to be filled with cheers that never came.

Mark's place remained conspicuously empty, a silent testament to his ailment, as he was confined to his bed, too unwell to partake in the festivities. In an attempt to bring some Christmas spirit to him, I carried his dinner and wrapped presents to his bedroom, hoping to brighten his spirits. Yet, despite my efforts, both the meal and gifts remained untouched, a poignant reminder of the severity of his condition on a day that should have been filled with warmth and laughter. The contrast between the festive setting and Mark's absence underscored the seriousness of his illness, turning a day of celebration into one of concern and reflection on what truly matters.

The first day the general practitioner's (GP) office reopened following the holiday season, I found myself eagerly awaiting a call back from a doctor, a call that quickly escalated into an unexpected deadlock. In a fervent attempt to secure the medical attention Mark so desperately needed, I found myself insisting on a home visit, given Mark's severe condition that left him too frail to even consider leaving the house. Contrarily, the doctor on the line was adamant that we bring Mark to the GP surgery, creating a frustrating loop of back-and-forth arguments.

This circular conversation reached a sudden and unsettling halt when the phone line abruptly went dead. This interruption came just after my husband had taken over the phone, his words "My wife is not being rude; she is simply requesting a home visit for her sick brother. I will report you to the Department of Health," still hanging in the air. The sudden silence was shocking, leaving us to wonder about the abrupt end to our plea for help. The doctor later claimed it was a mere disconnection, a claim that did little to ease the tension of the moment.

Our request for assistance had been made in the early hours, yet it wasn't until the late evening that we heard a knock at our door. To our surprise and relief, it was the very doctor we had spoken with earlier, arriving to finally examine Mark. This unexpected visit, though delayed, was a pivotal moment in addressing Mark's health concerns, coming after a day filled with anxiety and a desperate plea for medical intervention.

Navigating Mark's illness proved to be a challenging journey, especially with his reluctance to seek medical attention despite his deteriorating health. My determination to help him led to a series of appointments at both the hospital and the GP's office, all of which I arranged and attended alongside him. Throughout this time, there was a lingering hope that his symptoms, which we presumed were merely indicative of acid reflux, especially given his significant weight loss, would be manageable. However, this hope was based on a misunderstanding of the gravity of his condition.

The turning point came on April 13, 2017, the day before Good Friday, when an unavoidable work commitment prevented me from accompanying Mark to one of his appointments. My mother stepped in to accompany him to the hospital for an endoscopy, a procedure we hoped would offer some insight into his persistent symptoms. It was during this visit, in my absence, that the trajectory of Mark's health took a drastic and unforeseen turn.

The results of the endoscopy revealed a devastating truth far removed from the initial diagnosis of acid reflux: Mark was diagnosed with terminal cancer of the oesophagus, a revelation that blindsided us all. I received this heart-breaking news upon returning home from work, a moment that was etched in my memory with profound sadness. The weight of the diagnosis brought me to a state of overwhelming grief, marked by floods of tears, as the reality of Mark's condition and the magnitude of the battle ahead began to sink in.

In the wake of Mark's terminal diagnosis, I took on the mantle of his primary caregiver, a role made all the more crucial given our mother's advanced age, being in her late 70s. Our shared living situation facilitated my ability to closely monitor and attend to his needs. Recognising the importance of his comfort during such a trying time, I invested in a new mattress, ensuring that his resting hours were as peaceful as possible. To help occupy his mind and provide some distraction from his condition, I gifted him an iPad, hoping it would offer some semblance of normalcy and enjoyment.

Understanding the challenges Mark faced with eating, I sought out nutritional solutions that could support his health without requiring solid food intake. I purchased Ensure drinks in bulk, which are rich in essential vitamins and minerals, to sustain him nutritionally since he was unable to consume traditional food. Despite these efforts and the placement of a stent to aid in bypassing the tumour obstructing his oesophagus, the cancer's relentless spread to other organs was a stark indicator that our time with Mark was diminishing rapidly. The onset of yellow jaundice was a visible sign of his worsening condition, marking the progression of his illness.

The final stages of Mark's journey saw him admitted to the Royal Berkshire Hospital in Reading, before a necessary transfer to the Duchess of Kent Hospice. I accompanied him in the ambulance on that poignant day, Saturday, 27th May 2017. Arriving at the hospice, the emotional toll of the situation overwhelmed me, leading to an outpour of grief as I grappled with the impending loss of my brother. In that moment of profound sorrow, a compassionate Sue Ryder nurse offered me comfort through a simple yet powerful gesture of a reassuring hug. Her empathy in the face of my heartbreak was a small beacon of light during one of my darkest times.

Even as I confronted the reality of Mark's approaching end, I clung to one final hope—to fulfil his wish of seeing the seaside once more, a nostalgic reminiscence of our cherished childhood memories in Skegness. With this in mind, I discussed the possibility with the palliative care doctor, who supported the idea as a meaningful goal to pursue. This plan, albeit small in the grand scheme, represented a heartfelt attempt to bring joy to Mark's final days, an endeavour to create one last beautiful memory together.

On Sunday, 28th May 2017, in an effort to bring a moment of joy to Mark during his final days, I brought Smokey, my cat, to visit him at the hospice. Smokey, a beautiful Norwegian Forest cat with striking emerald green eyes, had always shared a special bond with Mark. She seemed to intuitively understand his condition, often following him closely during his times at home between hospital stays. Despite Mark's love for animals, this visit was different; he was in a sleep-like state, likely due to the medication administered to ease his pain and discomfort. Unable to interact with him, and with Smokey appearing uneasy in the unfamiliar environment, the visit was short-lived, lasting about 10 minutes before my husband took her back home.

Unaware that Mark's time was rapidly drawing to a close, I made the decision to stay with him through the night at the hospice. Seeking to create a serene and comforting atmosphere, I adorned his room with fresh flowers, their fragrance filling the space with a sense of tranquility. I also brought in a radio, setting it to play softly in the background, as music had always been something Mark enjoyed. The nurse on duty even remarked on the pleasant ambiance of the room, noting how lovely it both looked and smelled.

In the early hours of Monday, 29th May, around 5 a.m., the doctor urged me to bring our mother to the hospice immediately, as Mark's condition had taken a turn for the worse. When she arrived, we each took one of Mark's hands into our own, offering comfort and presence in his final moments. Mark passed away at 8:10 a.m. that Monday, leaving us in a state of profound loss.

The following day, Tuesday, 30th May, was my 49th birthday, making the timing of Mark's passing particularly poignant as he died just a day before. Adding to the confluence of significant dates, the funeral was scheduled for 14th June 2017, coincidentally falling on my wedding anniversary. This series of events intertwined personal milestones and grief in a deeply emotional way, marking a period of my life with both love and loss, forever remembered and felt with each passing year.

Chapter Twelve

The Last Time

The loss of my mother on Friday, 4th June 2021, at 7:30 p.m. due to ischemic heart disease was a profound shock to us. In the year leading up to her demise, she experienced several falls that necessitated the assistance of ambulance crews. However, her heart condition remained undiagnosed; we were aware of her severe osteoarthritis and mild cognitive impairment, but the revelation that she succumbed to a heart attack—mirroring the cause of her own mother's passing—was unexpected and deeply unsettling.

Her departure was particularly bewildering because it followed closely on the heels of her discharge from the hospital on Wednesday, 2nd June 2021, with a diagnosis as benign as constipation. This discharge came despite my own observations and call to emergency services, during which I reported symptoms that seemed indicative of a heart-related issue. This oversight raised numerous questions about the medical care she received and the apparent inability of her doctors to recognise the severity of her heart condition.

In the wake of these events, a post-mortem examination was conducted to ascertain the exact cause of her death. This step was deemed necessary due to the discrepancy between her symptoms, the lack of a clear diagnosis prior to her passing, and the need for clarity and understanding of what had truly happened. The outcome of the post-mortem was awaited with a mix of anxiety and a desperate need for closure, as we hoped to understand the circumstances that led to such a sudden and tragic loss.

The week leading up to my birthday in 2021 brought with it a haunting echo of the past, reminiscent of the experiences surrounding my grandmother's passing.

On Friday, 28th May, after I returned from work, my mother shared with me a profound and unsettling conversation she believed she had had with my late brother, her son Mark, who had passed away years earlier. This revelation was both startling and deeply moving, considering the significance of such encounters in our family history.

She described seeing Mark dressed in the smart black trousers and lovely green shirt in which he had been cremated, a detail that struck me with its vividness and specificity. When she recounted asking him if she was going to die and receiving no reply, the weight of her words hung heavily in the air. It seemed as if, in her own way, my mother was grappling with her mortality, echoing the premonitory moments my grandmother experienced before her own death.

This conversation occurred as my birthday, on Sunday, 30th May, was drawing near, adding another layer of emotional complexity to the days leading up to it. The message my mother wrote in my birthday card that year took on a new depth of meaning under the shadow of these events.

Her words, "To the best daughter in the whole world I love so much I never want to leave you. A very Happy Birthday and loads more. I was lucky when you were born to me, Donna. I love you so much Mum XXXXXXXXXXXXXXXX," now hold a place of cherished significance in my heart.

Her message, imbued with love and a poignant sense of premonition, became a treasured memory, a reminder of our bond and the profound, sometimes inexplicable, connections that can exist between loved ones. It underscored the delicate balance between life and death, love and loss, and the enduring strength of familial ties that transcend the physical realm.

The final moments I spent with my mother before her passing were tinged with a deceptive sense of normalcy, as she appeared to be in high spirits during my last visit to her at the Royal Berkshire Hospital. Despite the presence of an oxygen tank by her bed, a silent herald of the severity of her condition, she maintained her characteristic humour, bringing laughter to the hospital staff. This semblance of well-being, however, did not fully assuage my concerns, evident from the oxygen tank's silent presence.

Leaving the hospital that late afternoon, there were no overt signs that tragedy was imminent, prompting me to focus on preparations for her return home. I ventured to Morrison's to stock up on her favourite foods, envisioning a warm welcome back. This act of care was shadowed by a deep fatigue, compounded by the stress of continuously phoning the hospital throughout the night to check on her. The restrictions imposed by COVID-19 meant I couldn't be by her side, leaving me to rely on the updates from hospital staff.

Reflecting on her condition when she was initially taken by ambulance—her blue lips, the pallor of her skin, and her chilling coldness—it was clear she was in a critical state. The oxygen provided by the ambulance crew had offered a momentary relief, yet it was not enough to overcome the silent battle she was fighting.

The news of her passing at 7:30 p.m. came as a profound shock, especially as my husband and I arrived at the hospital shortly before 8 p.m., too late for a final goodbye. The depth of my devastation was mirrored by the emotional response of the hospital's staff; the junior doctors had been moved to tears by her unexpected departure. In her brief time at the hospital, my mother had left an indelible mark on the medical team, a testament to her resilient and jovial spirit despite a lifetime of profound challenges.

Her death was not only a personal tragedy but also a moment of poignant reflection on the impact she had on those around her, leaving a legacy of strength, warmth, and an unbreakable spirit that had endeared her to everyone she encountered, including the medical staff who had cared for her in her final days.

The farewell to my mother was marked by a blend of tradition and personal touches that reflected her essence and the deep connection we shared. The funeral began with a traditional church service, a nod to the values and faith that had been a cornerstone of her life. This was followed by a cremation service, mirroring the arrangements we had made for Mark, my brother, underscoring the continuity of family traditions in times of farewell.

In homage to her and as a symbol of our love and remembrance, we released 30 lilac balloons into the sky, a shift from the green balloons we had chosen for Mark, each colour deeply symbolic of the individual it represented. Additionally, the release of two white doves from a woven love heart basket, adorned with a lilac ribbon, added a poignant visual metaphor for peace and the journey of her spirit. The choice of lilac, in particular, resonated with her love for the garden, a space she had cultivated with passion and dedication.

The procession included a black hearse and a black limousine for immediate family members, maintaining the dignity and solemnity of the occasion. My mother's love for her expansive garden, a quarter of an acre of lush greenery, inspired the decision to host the wake in this cherished space. To accommodate guests and honour her in a manner she would have appreciated, I arranged for a large black marquee and hired a catering team to manage the food, ensuring that the wake was a fitting tribute to her life and legacy.

The impact of my mother's passing was profound, a shift in

the landscape of my existence that plunged me into a deep, all-encompassing state of bereavement depression. The intensity of the sorrow was such that it rendered me incapable of returning to work for nearly three months, as the very act of carrying on with day-to-day activities felt impossible, a betrayal of the depth of my loss.

During this period, the depth of my despair reached such a point that I harboured thoughts of joining her, driven by an overwhelming longing to care for her as I had always done. This wasn't simply a desire to escape the pain; it was more complex, intertwined with the roles of caregiver and daughter that had defined so much of my identity. The thought of her alone, even in death, was unbearable, highlighting the profound and unbreakable bond we shared, a connection that transcended the mere physical and ventured into the deeply spiritual.

This period of intense grief not only highlighted the unique and irreplaceable nature of our relationship but also left a gaping void in my life, a chasm that seemed to widen with each passing day. Her absence was felt in every quiet moment, every family gathering that echoed with her silence, and every life decision I faced without her wisdom and guidance. It was a testament to the indelible mark she had made on my heart and the profound influence she had on my life.

Navigating a world without her physical presence became my greatest challenge, a journey through uncharted territory where each step forward was a battle against the tide of my own sorrow. This experience forced me to confront the realities of grief and loss, to acknowledge the depth of my feelings and the necessity of facing them head-on. It was a painful yet crucial part of my healing process, teaching me invaluable lessons about love, loss, and the resilience of the human spirit.

In the wake of her passing, I learned that mourning is not an illness to be cured but a natural response to profound loss. It taught me the importance of self-compassion, of allowing myself to grieve fully and without shame, and of seeking support when the weight of my sorrow became too heavy to bear alone. This journey through grief was not just about learning to live without her but also about honouring her memory by embracing life with the same strength, love, and compassion that she exemplified every day.

Chapter Thirteen

The End

In the grand tapestry of human experience, few conditions are as misunderstood and as enigmatic as Bipolar Affective Disorder (BPAD). Known for its dramatic mood swings from the soaring heights of mania to the crushing depths of depression, BPAD is a severe, yet enduring mental health condition. However, like navigating a ship through stormy seas, with the right self-management strategies and support, one can steer towards a reasonably normal and fulfilling life.

My journey has been nothing short of a rollercoaster ride, marked by intense emotions, challenging periods of adjustment, and profound moments of self-discovery. Yet, despite the turbulence, I remain steadfastly optimistic about the future. This optimism is not born out of naivety but out of resilience; it is the light that guides me through the darkest nights and the anchor that grounds me during the highest tides.

Living with Bipolar Affective Disorder has taught me the importance of balance and self-awareness. It has forced me to confront my limitations and to recognise the value of self-care, medication, therapy, and a strong support network. These elements form the cornerstone of my self-management strategy, enabling me to lead a life that is as close to "normal" as possible.

The transition from working in the intensive care ward to my current role in CCTV Surveillance and Police Liaison at Prospect Park Psychiatric Hospital in the summer of 2023 was a significant milestone in my journey. This change was not just a shift in job roles but a strategic move to create a healthier work-life balance and reduce occupational stressors. It was a decision fuelled by self-awareness and a deep understanding of my health needs.

Working at the hospital, even in a different capacity, has allowed me to maintain a sense of purpose and connection to the community. It has given me a unique perspective on the human condition and the various forms of suffering and resilience I witness daily. This experience has enriched my empathy and understanding, not only for others but also for myself.

My story is one of many in the vast ocean of those living with Bipolar Affective Disorder. It is a testament to the fact that while BPAD is a part of our lives, it does not define us. We are captains of our own ships, navigating through the bipolar seas, sometimes sailing smoothly, other times braving the storms. But always moving forward, always hopeful for the dawn that follows even the darkest night.

As I look to the future, I am reminded that the journey of self-discovery and management of BPAD is ongoing. There will be challenges ahead, but there will also be triumphs. With each day, I learn more about myself, my disorder, and how to live a life that is not just about surviving but thriving.

In sharing my story, I hope to illuminate the path for others, to offer a beacon of hope and understanding in a world that often stigmatises and misunderstands mental illness. For anyone navigating the complex waters of Bipolar Affective Disorder, know that you are not alone. With the right support and self-management strategies, it is possible to lead a fulfilling, balanced, and optimistic life.

That's what I think my husband, Hassan, has been for me; the right support. His unwavering love and never-ending encouragement has guided me like a beacon of light. He has been there for me in the darkest of times and never did his resolve ever falter when it came to his family.

This kind of dedication I noticed when I saw him interact with Leila for the first time. The amount of love this man had for his child and how he could find it in himself to just keep giving and giving, first to his family, then to me when I entered his life. For someone who is such a giver, it shocks me to my core when I learn about the life he came from, all the things he had seen since he was a child and how different his childhood has been as compared to a lot of us who grew up with less but still had each other. It gives me an opportunity to reflect on all my feelings against my family and my time with Tony.

My affection for my husband remains unwavering, despite the numerous obstacles we have encountered side by side. The vows I pronounced in the sacred ambiance of the church, committing to "In sickness and in health, till death us do part," resonate within me as profoundly now as they did over two decades ago.

Our origins are starkly different, each marked by its own form of volatility, which has only served to strengthen our bond. I hail from England, a backdrop that has shaped my story as detailed in this memoir. My husband, Hassan, comes from a war-ravaged Palestine in the Middle East, a region beset by conflict and turmoil. His life story, equally filled with unimaginable hardships, remains untold, a true narrative awaiting its voice.

Intriguingly, this memoir paves the way for a forthcoming book, "Right to Return", which will delve deeper into Hassan's life in Palestine, the conflict he endured, and his journey to England. This anticipated work promises to shed light on his profound experiences and the resilience he has shown throughout his life. Together, these diverse histories have not only tested our resilience but have also deepened our understanding and love for each other.

About the Author

Donna was told by many friends she should write a memoir about her unimaginable life story and fulfilling a life-long-dream Donna put pen to paper to accomplish that goal.

Never shying from the harrowing truths of living with Bipolar, experiencing psychosis and attempting to take her own life, Donna`s story is not written to shock or sensationalise. Rather, her aim is to inspire others, who have experienced such terrifying delusions and overwhelming lows to believe that whatever is being felt at a particular moment in time, careful management of a mental health condition can deliver transformative change.

Donna`s goal is to share her true tragic story to the world to help others in similar circumstances or just purely to educate the many diverse disadvantaged topics covered by her memoir.

Donna currently works at the local psychiatric hospital in Reading, Berkshire where she was previously an inpatient.